The New York Times

COFFEE AND CROSSWORDS: MOCHA MONDAY

The New York Times

COFFEE AND CROSSWORDS: MOCHA MONDAY
75 Very Easy Monday Puzzles from *The New York Times*

Edited by Will Shortz

ST. MARTIN'S GRIFFIN ☙ NEW YORK

The New York Times

COFFEE AND CROSSWORDS: MOCHA MONDAY

ACROSS

1 "___ upon a time . . ."
5 Like a score of 10 out of 10
10 Speedy
14 "Star Wars" princess
15 Dated yet trendy
16 Knowing of
17 "See you again!"
20 Longtime CBS and NBC newsman Roger
21 Touchdown destination
22 Blacktops
25 Tricky curves
27 Bud's partner in comedy
28 Had dinner
29 ___ B'rith
30 Coarse file
31 "Veni, vidi, vici" speaker
34 The "R" of NPR
37 "See you again!"
41 Henry Blake's rank on "M*A*S*H": Abbr.
42 Many I.M. recipients
44 Letterhead design
47 "___ Green" (Kermit the Frog song)
49 Snooze
50 In the style of
51 Mah-jongg pieces
53 Domineering
55 The dole
57 Chief Norse deity
59 "See you again!"
64 Suffix with sock
65 Ship-related
66 Lawman Wyatt
67 Former Cub ___ Sandberg
68 Entrap
69 Where "you can do whatever you feel," in a hit 1978 song

DOWN

1 Outdated
2 Recent: Prefix
3 The Reds, on scoreboards
4 Words on a Wonderland cake
5 Steamed
6 Muffle, as a sound
7 U.F.O. fliers
8 Kind of well
9 Michaels of "Saturday Night Live"
10 "Happy Days" cool cat, with "the"
11 Country north of Namibia
12 Dictation takers
13 Shredded
18 Greyhound vehicle
19 TV spots
22 Grp. funding 19-Down in campaigns
23 Just slightly
24 Swerve
26 "Nobody doesn't like" her, in a slogan
29 ___-a-brac
30 Stir up
32 Lindbergh's classic flight, e.g.
33 Fitting
35 Actress Cannon
36 "How was ___ know?"
38 Duke or earl
39 Restroom door word
40 Chapters in history
43 Austin Powers, e.g.
44 Perry Mason, e.g.
45 Clinton cabinet member Hazel
46 Gasoline unit
48 Weather map line
51 Tic-___-toe
52 Cattle branding tools
53 Lighter and pen maker
54 Perfectly pitched
56 A polar bear might be found on one
58 Valley
60 Actress Mendes
61 '60s conflict site
62 Tolkien creature
63 F.D.R. initiative

by Dave and Tracy Mackey

2

ACROSS

1 Black-bordered news item
5 Anne of "Wag the Dog"
10 Dull-colored
14 Internet connection at a restaurant or airport
15 Fanfare
16 Seized vehicle
17 Snoop
19 Height: Prefix
20 Steak that a dog might end up with
21 "Huckleberry Finn" author
22 Wet mascara worry
25 Felix and Oscar, with "the"
28 Bathroom powder
30 Wyatt of the Wild West
31 Magazine V.I.P.'s
32 1980s video game with a maze
35 Down, usually, on a light switch
38 Carouse
42 Golf peg
43 Boxed stringed instrument
44 "___ solemnly swear . . ."
45 Ax or awl
47 Judicial assertion
49 Symbol of purity
54 Figure of speech
55 Wall art
56 Mutual of ___
58 "Gotcha," to a beatnik
59 Want ad heading . . . or a hint to the starts of 17-, 25-, 38- and 49-Across
64 Queue
65 More than steamed
66 March Madness org.
67 Brain readings, for short
68 Parceled (out)
69 Safecracker

DOWN

1 To have and to hold
2 Life story, for short
3 Conditions
4 Men's fashion accessory
5 Submarine sandwich
6 Commercial prefix with Lodge
7 Informed, with "in"
8 ___ Solo of "Star Wars"
9 Flight board info: Abbr.
10 Use, as past experience
11 CliffsNotes version
12 "___ Love," 1957 #1 hit by 13-Down
13 Singer Pat
18 Brusque
21 The Blue Jays, on a scoreboard
22 Rung
23 Furious with
24 Pitcher of milk?
26 John Donne's "___ Be Not Proud"
27 Went by dugout
29 Passover bread
33 Spicy dish that may have a fire-alarm rating
34 Encountered
36 ___-Lay (snack company)
37 At the end of one's patience
39 Take-home pay
40 Squirm
41 Capitol's top
46 Bird that hoots
48 Crevice
49 Photographer's request
50 Peep show flick
51 Circular gasket
52 Go ___ for (support in time of need)
53 Overact
57 Copied
59 Huck's raftmate
60 Metal from a mine
61 Sno-cone filler
62 Re-re-re-remind
63 Respond to a really bad joke, maybe

by Ken Bessette

3

ACROSS

1. Bounce to the surface
6. Botch
10. Sports equipment
14. Belittle
15. Least bit
16. Present opener?
17. Free health and dental care, and then some
20. List of test answers
21. Aviates
22. Limerick or sonnet
23. Luke's twin sister in "Star Wars"
24. Price ___ pound
25. Math symbol for extraction of a root
30. Pilot's stat.
33. Warnings
34. Entree in a bowl with beef or lamb, say
36. Pelvic bones
37. Boat propeller
38. Clark's crush on "Smallville"
39. "Hey, come back a bit"
42. Enter en masse
44. Where pigs wallow
45. In limbo
47. Wood-shaping tool
48. Nays' opposites
49. Flair
52. Peppermint ___ of "Peanuts"
54. Sombrero, e.g.
57. Eyeglass option for different distances
60. Early state in the presidential campaign
61. Reclined
62. Major artery
63. The Big Board: Abbr.
64. Doe's mate
65. Winona of "Girl, Interrupted"

DOWN

1. Pitcher's faux pitch
2. New York theater award
3. One often needing a change
4. Take advantage of
5. "Couldn't be better!"
6. Pertaining to a son or daughter
7. Ear or leaf part
8. Four Corners-area Indians
9. Prohibition
10. Errand runner
11. Dubai dignitary
12. Six-legged scurriers
13. Move skyward
18. Fake identity
19. Occurrence
23. Bygone Italian coins
24. Tour grp.?
25. Monsoon occurrences
26. Apportion
27. God or goddess
28. Brainy
29. Suffix with bombard
30. Trailblazing video game maker
31. His tomb is in Red Square
32. Banjo sound
35. Hits hard
37. Lummox
40. Like 16 vis-à-vis 15, agewise
41. Turk's topper
42. Home viewing for a price
43. Subscription period, often
46. Loathing
47. Aquatic plant life
49. Pirouette
50. "Iliad" setting
51. Cries after being burned
52. H.S. junior's exam
53. Where most of Russia is
54. Group of buffalo
55. Prefix with chamber
56. Ruler before 31-Down
58. Ernie of the 24-Down
59. Silver screen star Myrna

by Lynn Lempel

4

ACROSS

1 Boston orchestra
5 Seaboard
10 30 minutes, in the N.F.L.
14 Once more
15 God of the Koran
16 Mixed bag
17 X-rated dance
19 Miniature plateau
20 Top secret?
21 "Thar ___ blows!"
22 Something to cram for
23 Banjo picker Scruggs
25 Org. that publishes American Hunter
27 Some Caribbean music
30 Beach find
36 Referred to
39 ___ Speedwagon (1970s–'80s band)
40 Rotgut
41 "___ of Two Cities"
42 Fabergé collectible
43 Acquire, as a debt
44 ___ badge, boy scout's award
45 Dover's state: Abbr.
46 ___ jacket, 1960s fashion
47 Initial power source
50 One of a D.C. 100
51 401(k) alternative, for short
52 Oodles
55 Object of the actions suggested by the starts of 17-, 30-, 47- and 66-Across
58 "You've ___ Mail"
61 Lose all one's money in gambling
65 Thomas Edison's middle name
66 Pinto
68 Plane assignment
69 Ryan of "The Beverly Hillbillies"
70 Julia Roberts's role in "Ocean's Eleven"
71 Golfer's target
72 Krupp Works city
73 Alphabetize, e.g.

DOWN

1 It might be checkered
2 Not fooled by
3 Llama country
4 Slide, as a credit card through a reader
5 Supplies, as food for a party
6 Cheer for El Cordobés
7 "Ah, me!"
8 Part of a girl scout's uniform
9 Finis
10 1990 Macaulay Culkin film
11 The "A" in A-Rod
12 Kudrow of "Friends"
13 Cappuccino head
18 ___ brain (nitwit)
24 "Streets of ___" (classic cowboy song)
26 Bird that comes "bob, bob, bobbin'"
27 Little rascal
28 Ben Franklin, famously, in an electrical storm
29 Arcade game maker
31 Israeli desert
32 Sharp turn on a golf course
33 Sources of Scottish streams
34 Sky-blue
35 Twice-seen TV show
37 Competitor of "The 5th Wheel," in reality TV
38 Scare off
48 Chatterbox
49 Spoiled
53 Scrooge's cry
54 Dalmatian markings
55 Launder
56 Margarine
57 White House office shape
59 Crew's control?
60 Deadlocks
62 Cookie with a creme center
63 Stalingrad's land, for short
64 The "T" of S.A.T.
67 U-turn from SSW

by Randall J. Hartman

ACROSS

1 ___ Antoinette
6 Tallies
10 Series of scenes
13 Actress Blake or Plummer
15 Not having a stitch on
16 Letter before sigma
17 Lump in the throat
18 "Calm down!"
20 Neighbor of Scot.
21 Dabbling duck
23 Years and years and years
24 "Move!"
29 One-named Art Deco master
30 Stephen of "The Crying Game"
31 Bear in constellation names
34 Cap or helmet
39 "Pay attention!"
43 Cared for a home while the owner was away
44 Pink wine
45 Hang back
46 Sail support
49 "Lookie there!"
56 Like many a wiseacre's comment: Abbr.
57 Part of F.Y.I.
58 Lots of laughs
60 "Oh, be serious!"
64 Car model with a musical name
66 Metalliferous rock
67 Done with
68 Passes, as a law
69 Auction motion
70 Farewells
71 "Savvy?"

DOWN

1 Crew member
2 Honor ___ thieves
3 Poconos or Tetons
4 Write-___ (some votes)
5 Manuscript receiver
6 White, in Mexico
7 Owing
8 Banned insecticide
9 Caribbean, e.g.
10 "This way" sign
11 Dishes for fancy meals
12 ___-turvy
14 Native seal hunter
19 "Golly!"
22 Breakfasted, e.g.
25 Parts of an udder
26 Stew
27 Go like mad
28 "If I ___ hammer . . ."
31 "Yuck!"
32 Rock's ___ Speedwagon
33 Sutcliffe of the early Beatles
34 F.D.R. successor
35 Middle measurement
36 It may be puffed up
37 Sighs of contentment
38 Letter carrier's assignment: Abbr.
40 Hades
41 Golfer ___ Aoki
42 Heroic legend
46 Call to a calf
47 Blow ___ (become enraged)
48 Brawny
49 Not be able to swallow
50 When to celebrate el año nuevo
51 Schlepped
52 "Gimme ___!" (frequent Alabama cheerleader's cry)
53 Color specialists
54 "It's ___" ("There's no doubt")
55 ___-frutti
59 Cartoonist Thomas
61 High tennis shot
62 Some Christmas greenery
63 Doctor's quote
65 Scottish refusal

by C. W. Stewart

6

ACROSS

1 Stars and Stripes, e.g.
5 Places where lines meet
9 French greeting
14 ___ of Sandwich
15 Cause of a game cancellation
16 Unaccompanied
17 "Here he is now!"
20 Black card
21 Talks one's head off
22 French summer
23 Twinings selections
26 Sign before Virgo
27 Big Apple ave.
28 Be undecided
33 ___ Wednesday
34 Suds maker
35 Mounted, as a horse
38 Talking maybe a little too fast
40 Snapshot
43 Sgt. Snorkel's dog
44 Fable writer
46 No. on which a magazine's ad rates are based
48 Freudian one
49 Persist to completion
53 Prefix with center
55 Column's counterpart
56 Interstate entrance or exit
57 Fish after which a cape is named
58 Logic diagram
60 Long Island airfield town
64 Command center? . . . or where you might hear the starts of 17-, 28- and 49-Across

68 Nephew of Donald Duck
69 For whom the bell tolls, in a John Donne meditation
70 Numerical prefix with -ber
71 Bygone Montreal ball club
72 Quiet exercise
73 Remove from the freezer

DOWN

1 Admit (to), with "up"
2 Reindeer herder
3 Geometry calculation
4 "My pleasure"
5 Black power hairdo, for short
6 Dunderpate
7 The "C" in N.Y.C.
8 Divided 50-50
9 Dirge
10 Schooner fill
11 Billet-doux
12 Join
13 Old message system
18 Wails
19 Dueling sword
24 Perched on
25 Deposed Iranian
28 "Roots," for one
29 ___ of Wight
30 Message on a shipping crate
31 Geologic time unit
32 Pigeon's sound
36 Big elevator manufacturer
37 ___ too soon
39 Droid

41 Wedding cake feature
42 Killer whale
45 Republican, Democratic, Green, etc.
47 "Luann" or "Blondie"
50 Knight time?
51 A score
52 End result
53 French place of learning
54 Mail receiver, in brief
59 Repeat
61 ___ Ness monster
62 Itsy-bitsy bit
63 Winter truck attachment
65 God, in Italy
66 Brain scan, for short
67 Bounding main

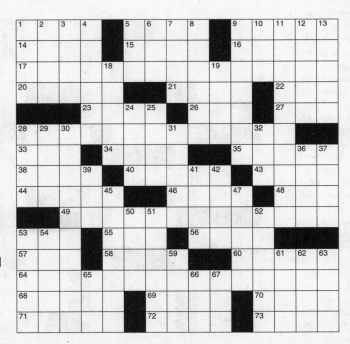

by Ken Bessette

ACROSS

1 "I saw ___ sawing wood . . ." (old tongue twister)
5 Lawn base
8 Finally
14 Outlaws
15 "I won! I won!," e.g.
16 Amp toter
17 What President Washington said upon winning the lottery?
19 Professor's goal
20 "I've got a mule, her name is ___"
21 Once around the sun
22 Hidden valley
23 What flagmaker Ross said . . . ?
28 Colonial Franklin, familiarly
29 Cheer to a matador
30 Just watched
33 What Miss Molly said . . . ?
39 End in ___ (draw)
40 In a huff
41 Captain who said "Eat your pudding, Mr. Land"
42 What Galileo said . . . ?
44 "I can't ___ satisfaction" (Rolling Stones lyric)
45 "___ shocked . . . SHOCKED!"
46 Collide
47 What the Big Bad Wolf said . . . ?
55 Figure skater's jump
56 Rocklike
57 Clamor
59 Overhaul

62 What Noah Webster said . . . ?
64 Aftershock
65 Shepherd's locale
66 Nylons
67 High-school honey
68 Directional suffix
69 Ready for business

DOWN

1 Flows out
2 Request at a medical exam
3 Viewpoint
4 Put to good ___
5 Porch protector
6 "Rock of Ages" accompaniment
7 Hair colorers
8 Picasso output
9 Little piggy
10 Actress Jessica
11 Rated NC-17, e.g.
12 Fathers
13 Wee
18 Hand-wringer's words
24 Monk's home
25 Traffic noises
26 Merrie ___ England
27 Command to Rover
30 ___ Miguel, largest island of the Azores
31 Part of N.C.A.A.: Abbr.
32 Actor Robbins
33 Commercial prefix with phone
34 Row
35 "You're ___ talk!"

36 Rent out
37 Trio after K
38 "___-hoo!"
40 Slanted type: Abbr.
43 Sis or bro
44 Lightheaded
46 Novelist Melville
47 Witches' blemishes
48 Put forth, as effort
49 Flood stopper
50 Transporter across the Andes
51 Not cut up
52 HBO's "Real Time With Bill ___"
53 Lottery winner's yell
54 Convalescent home employee
58 Biblical place of innocence
60 Hip, in the '60s
61 Delve (into)
63 "Sez ___?"

by C. W. Stewart

8

ACROSS

1 Ooze
5 La ___, Milan opera house
10 One-spot cards
14 "Not guilty," e.g.
15 Jeopardy
16 Phileas ___, who went around the world in 80 days
17 Like 39-Across's fans on his induction day?
19 Plenty
20 Uses a stool
21 Spy Mata ___
23 Warmongers
26 H.S. junior's exam
28 Old horse
31 Away from the wind
32 Layers
34 Letter before omega
35 "___ Bitsy Spider"
36 Waved one's arms at, as a cab
37 Place to wager on the 28-Acrosses: Abbr.
38 Goes bad, as fruit
39 Notable Army inductee of 3/24/58
40 Military no-show
41 Part of a gearwheel
42 Flexible
43 Land of Lima and llamas
44 French "a"
45 Makes very happy
46 Balletic bend
47 ___ and feather
48 Simplicity
49 Legendary Chicago Bears coach George
50 Singer ___ Anthony
52 One who makes a good first impression?
54 Derrière
56 Last movie 39-Across made before his Army stint

62 Dunce cap, geometrically
63 1975–78 U.S. Open champ Chris
64 Finger's end
65 Novelist Seton
66 Artist who liked to paint dancers
67 Hard journey

DOWN

1 Place to refresh oneself
2 Building wing
3 Wriggly swimmer
4 Openers for all doors
5 Good name for a Dalmatian
6 Corporate V.I.P.'s
7 Noah's ___
8 "Ally McBeal" actress Lucy
9 Some computer software checks
10 Light years away
11 Army officer who met 39-Across in 25-Down
12 Self-esteem
13 Last Army rank of 39-Across: Abbr.
18 What the "H" of H.M.S. may be
22 Not too much
23 Much-photographed event after 39-Across's induction
24 City with a Penn State campus
25 Where 39-Across was stationed overseas
26 First Army rank of 39-Across
27 Like seawater
29 Waldorf-___ Hotel

30 First movie 39-Across made after his Army stint
32 Defeated soundly
33 Actresses Shire and Balsam
40 Clear to all
42 Word before group or pressure
49 What the "H" of H.M.S. may be
51 Neighborhood
52 Indian tourist city
53 Police hdqrs.
54 Record label of 39-Across
55 Long, long time
57 "___ had it!"
58 Photo image, briefly
59 Rowboat mover
60 Made-up story
61 Antlered animal

by David J. Kahn

ACROSS

1 Sea creature that sidles
5 Group of eight musicians
10 Underhanded plan
14 Greeting in Granada
15 Get up
16 Toy block brand
17 Andy's partner in old radio
18 *Sci-fi barrier
20 *Newspaper article lead-in
22 Quenched
23 Big name in audio equipment
24 Martial artist Jackie
25 Result of a belly flop
28 *When the curtain goes up
32 Quiet spells
33 Bed board
34 Turf
35 Kind of history
36 Word that can precede each half of the answers to each of the eight starred clues
37 Performed ballads, e.g.
38 President pro ___
39 Go after bucks or ducks, say
40 Outpouring
41 *Wrestling move that puts an arm around someone's neck
44 Less bold
45 Slick
46 Corduroy ridge
47 Measly
50 *Secret communication location

54 *Mars Pathfinder, for one
56 Rouse from slumber
57 Regarding
58 Western flick, in old lingo
59 Farm measure
60 Abound (with)
61 One of a reporter's five W's
62 Annum

DOWN

1 Punched-out part of a paper ballot
2 Capital of Italia
3 Plenty
4 *Diamond game
5 Like a lout
6 Hag
7 Become bushed
8 PC bailout key

9 Golfer's opening drive
10 Flexible
11 Cousin of an onion
12 Gawk at
13 Sondheim's "Sweeney ___"
19 Scratch on a diamond, e.g.
21 Amount printed in red ink
24 Nautical map
25 Slow-moving mammal
26 Blender setting
27 South American wool source
28 Move with one's tail between one's legs
29 Actor and rockabilly crooner Chris

30 Three-card hustle
31 Yard worker's tool
33 Impertinent
37 *Indy 500 venue
39 "Yikes!"
40 Hawk, as wares
42 Business that may have gone boom and then bust in the '90s
43 Pre-euro money in 2-Down
44 ___ d'
46 Eucharist disk
47 H.S. junior's exam
48 Cathedral recess
49 Tardy
50 Corner, as a king
51 10K or marathon
52 Gumbo ingredient
53 House of Lords member
55 Pep squad shout

by Jeff Armstrong

ACROSS

1 See 48-Down
5 Stick in one's ___
9 Frank of the Mothers of Invention
14 Not loco
15 "___ and the King of Siam"
16 Decorate
17 Bess Truman or Barbara Bush
19 Snooped, with "about"
20 "You're ___ talk!"
21 Enclosure with a MS.
23 NNW's opposite
24 Hi-___ monitor
25 Question after the fact
29 Car bomb?
31 Old letter salutation
32 "God's Little ___" (Erskine Caldwell best seller)
34 Competitor of Dove or Camay
36 Prop for Picasso
40 Takes care of all possibilities
44 Pan-cooked brunch treat
45 Words after ". . . as long as you both shall live?"
46 "Mona ___"
47 Make the cut?
50 Funny DeGeneres
52 Grilling
56 "Shame on you!"
59 Crew's control?
60 One who indulges too much in the grape
61 French city famous for its mustard
63 Garbo of "Mata Hari," 1932
65 1990 Macaulay Culkin film
68 Ed of "Lou Grant"
69 The "U" in B.T.U.

70 Compete in the America's Cup
71 Bookcase part
72 Model Banks
73 Med school subj.

DOWN

1 In regard to
2 Where Bangor is
3 Put aside for later
4 Place for eggs
5 Iron Man Ripken of the Orioles
6 Genetic letters
7 ___ forth (et cetera)
8 Brother comic Shawn or Marlon
9 "Riders of the Purple Sage" author
10 Hullabaloo
11 Star's entourage
12 ". . . or ___ 1 for more options"
13 Peruvian peaks

18 Play with, as a Frisbee
22 Star Wars program, for short
26 Morays, e.g.
27 Hint
28 Fit to be tried?
30 More profound
32 U.N.C.'s athletic org.
33 Where streets intersect: Abbr.
35 "Sweet" age in ancient Rome?
37 Play by George Bernard Shaw
38 Superman's symbol
39 Meadow
41 Relatively low-temperature star
42 German river in a 1943 R.A.F. raid
43 Part to play
48 With 1-Across, infamous Ugandan dictator

49 Opposite of "At ease!"
51 Mother of Castor and Pollux
52 "Animal House" party costumes
53 Like winters in the Arctic
54 Ballroom dancer Castle
55 Foolish person, slangily
57 Braga of "Kiss of the Spider Woman"
58 Prepared to pray
62 She requested "As Time Goes By"
64 ___ Aviv
66 Bygone Russian space station
67 When a plane is due in: Abbr.

by Randall J. Hartman

ACROSS

1 Vampire's tooth
5 Playing marble
10 At any time
14 πr^2 for a circle
15 Engine
16 Lucy Lawless TV role
17 From ___ (completely)
18 Cheri formerly of "S.N.L."
19 Persia, today
20 Bidding impediment?
23 "Ooh, tasty!"
26 Enter
27 Streisand film about a Jewish girl masquerading as a boy
28 How sardines may be packed
30 Suffix with vocal
32 Enzyme suffix
33 Outdoor meal deterrent?
38 Gas brand with the slogan "Put a tiger in your tank"
39 Book after Daniel
40 Show ___ (attend, as a meeting)
44 Truth obstruction?
47 ___ Francisco
50 Inc., abroad
51 Lawn care brand
52 Garbage
54 Tipplers
57 The second "S" in MS-DOS: Abbr.
58 Metallic element's obstacle?
62 Small plateau
63 Singer Bryant
64 January to December
68 Humdinger
69 Odometer units
70 Nautilus captain
71 Chair or pew
72 Happening
73 Photo often taken after an accident

DOWN

1 Air safety org.
2 Murals and such
3 Opposite of paleo-
4 Mideast's ___ Strip
5 BP gas brand
6 Crime boss known as the Teflon Don
7 Had dinner at home
8 Bullring bull
9 "___ go bragh!"
10 Napoleon, on Elba or St. Helena
11 "The Two Gentlemen of ___"
12 Passes, as a law
13 Annoy
21 Aptly named tropical fruit
22 Computer memory unit
23 "Eek!"
24 Les États-___
25 Beaded shoes, informally
29 "Are you ___ out?"
30 "___ a man with seven wives"
31 Neuter
34 Casual conversation
35 Wrestling move
36 "___ live and breathe!"
37 German industrial valley
41 No ___ allowed (sign)
42 Hurting all over
43 Some boxing results
45 Grades 1 to 12, briefly
46 Mozart's "___ fan tutte"
47 Actor John of "Full House"
48 Dahl or Francis
49 Pregnancy symptom, frequently
53 Brainy
54 Photographer's request
55 Frequently
56 "Here's mud in your eye!," e.g.
59 Partner of rank and serial number
60 Prof's place: Abbr.
61 Wildcat
65 Suffix with musket
66 Doc's org.
67 Dodgers catcher Campanella

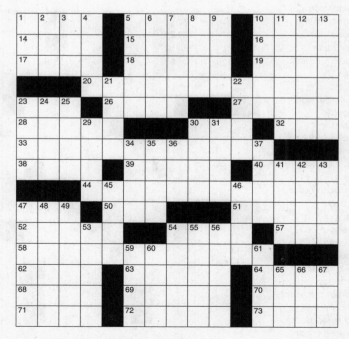

by Christina Houlihan Kelly

12

ACROSS

1 Do some fall farmwork
5 Servings of corn
9 Windshield material
14 Auto shaft
15 Ladder rung
16 Actor Murphy of old westerns
17 Twelvemonth
18 Symbol of a new start
20 Low-growing tree found typically in rocky soil
22 Joined by treaty
23 Tax org.
24 Actress Longoria
25 Byways: Abbr.
26 Dangerous cargo
30 Does the butterfly, e.g.
32 Fugard's "A Lesson From ___"
33 It indicates the seconds on a clock face
37 Aussie jumpers
38 Three squares, e.g.
39 ___ Lackawanna (bygone railroad)
40 Small whirlwind
42 Carpenter's tool
43 "As You Like It" forest
44 Ransacked and robbed
45 Seer's gift, briefly
48 It's about 78% nitrogen
49 Butterfly catcher
50 Hasty glance
52 Stock transaction done at a loss for tax purposes
57 Old radio part
59 "Stronger than dirt" sloganeer
60 Commerce on the Web
61 Out of harbor
62 Visitors to baby Jesus
63 Drug-yielding shrub
64 "Hey!"
65 Once, long ago

DOWN

1 Sunbeams
2 Prez or veep
3 Banned spray on apple trees
4 Lima's land
5 Debutante's date
6 Book of maps
7 Smell horrible
8 Fat farm
9 Old-fashioned light
10 Pause
11 Red who fought oil well fires
12 Put in place
13 Does some spring farmwork
19 Forces at sea
21 Favoritism or discrimination
24 Actor Tom of "The Girl Can't Help It"
26 Difficult
27 Baseball's Felipe or Jesus
28 Places with exotic animals
29 Legendary Washington hostess Perle ___
30 Lover
31 Bookcase part
33 Cut apart
34 Asia's ___ Sea
35 Three's opposite on a clock face
36 Land owner's document
38 Steak order
41 Bram Stoker novel
42 Central part
44 Usher again
45 Roof's edge
46 Sudden outpouring
47 Pie nut
49 Local theaters, in slang
51 Go to rack and ___
52 Pantywaist
53 Unchanged
54 Not quite closed
55 Doesn't keep up
56 Number on an Interstate sign
58 Faucet

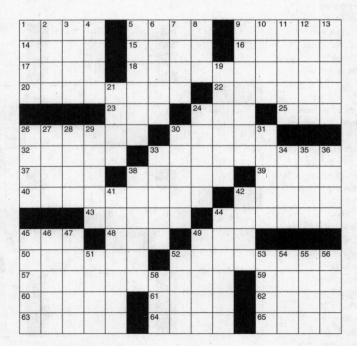

by Janet R. Bender

Note: 17- and 64-Across and 11- and 34-Down each conceals an article of clothing.

ACROSS

1 "Miss America" might be printed on one
5 Mafia bosses
10 "Ali ___ and the Forty Thieves"
14 Painterish
15 Japanese cartoons
16 Grandson of Adam
17 Boardinghouse sign
19 Perched on
20 Together
21 Canceled
22 Goes out in a game of rummy
23 Katmandu resident
25 Snarled mess
27 Old-time actress Turner
29 "Chill!"
32 Many conundrums have them
35 Sneak peek: Var.
39 Suffix with human or organ
40 Pitcher's stat
41 Making out . . . or a hint to this puzzle's four hidden articles of clothing
42 4:00 drink
43 Pages that aren't editorial matter
44 Open, as an envelope
45 Pod contents
46 Perfectly clear
48 Some creepy-crawlies
50 Vinegary
54 Slave
58 The "C" in T.L.C.
60 Openly declare
62 Eskimo home
63 ___ Romeo (car)
64 Halifax's home

66 Male-only
67 El ___, Spanish artist
68 Cooking fat
69 Sharpen, as skills
70 Church council
71 God of war

DOWN

1 Brand of kitchen wrap
2 Lifted off the launch pad, e.g.
3 Not stand completely erect
4 Church songbooks
5 Purrer
6 Soon, to poets
7 Stove light
8 Letter after phi, chi, psi
9 Not vacillating about

10 Snoopy, for one
11 Favoring common folk
12 Great benefit
13 Nile reptiles
18 Emmy-winning Ward
24 Permanently, as writing
26 Tour de France winner LeMond
28 Rainbow shapes
30 Between ports
31 Lennon/Ono's "Happy ___ (War Is Over)"
32 Sound of laughter
33 Language of Lahore
34 Daytona 500 enthusiast
36 ___ out a living
37 Lab bottle

38 Not yet burning
41 Michelangelo's David, e.g.
45 Shaded passageway
47 Time of advancing glaciers
49 À la mode
51 Zesty flavors
52 Old piano key material
53 Witches' group
55 Place to exchange "I do's"
56 Valley known for its chateaux
57 Laundry units
58 Bills and coins
59 Saxophone type
61 Texas city on the Brazos
65 Old prairie home material

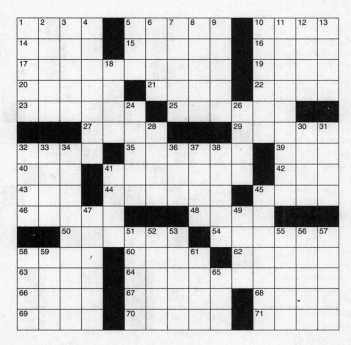

by Gary Disch

14

ACROSS

1 Meat featured in a Monty Python musical title
5 Alternatives to PC's
9 Popeye's creator E. C. ___
14 "Look what I did!"
15 "There oughta be ___!"
16 Singer Cara
17 Difficult burden
18 Many a stadium cover
19 Exxon competitor
20 Tourism bureau's offering
23 The matador's opponent
24 Totally cool, in '90s slang
25 Photo ___ (White House events)
28 It's swung at Wimbledon
32 J.F.K.'s successor
35 Ooze
36 1983 Barbra Streisand title role
37 Notes in a poker pot
39 It makes bread rise
42 Old-time wisdom
43 Kind of patch for a rabbit
45 Ark builder
47 Try to win, in romance
48 Pesky wasp
52 Communication means for the deaf: Abbr.
53 Cry when a light bulb goes on
54 Clears an Etch A Sketch, e.g.
58 It helps determine how much tax you owe the I.R.S.
62 Team leader
64 Venus de ___
65 Actress Spelling
66 Airs, in Latin
67 Suffix with switch
68 "The devil ___ the details"
69 King with a golden touch
70 Amount owed
71 Guitarist Atkins

DOWN

1 Vermont ski town
2 Group of experts
3 Like blue movies
4 Yale's bulldog, e.g.
5 Small amount of cash saved for an emergency
6 ___ vera
7 Pitch tents for the night
8 Says on a stack of Bibles
9 Time off from work with pay
10 Cleveland's lake
11 Become acquainted with
12 Lee who directed "Crouching Tiger, Hidden Dragon"
13 ___ Speedwagon
21 Miners' finds
22 Mercury or Saturn, but not Venus
26 Oil industry prefix
27 Canonized fifth-century pope
29 Born: Fr.
30 Classic toothpaste brand
31 Animation frame
32 Muammar el-Qaddafi's land
33 Makes yawn
34 Noted performing arts school
38 "My gal" of song
40 Party to the left of Dem.
41 Become established
44 Targets of Raid
46 Queen on Mount Olympus
49 A question of identity
50 Blocked, as radio broadcasts
51 Bit of strategy
55 Smidgen
56 Like "The Twilight Zone" music
57 Tour of duty
59 Univ. sports org.
60 Country whose name is an anagram of 10-Down
61 Unidentifiable mass
62 Film device, for short
63 Yves's yes

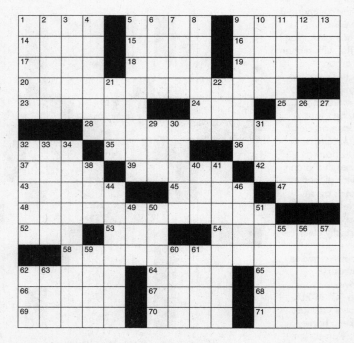

by Stella Daily and Bruce Venzke

ACROSS

1 Peeling knives
7 "See ya"
10 Katie Couric's network
13 Kansas city where Dwight Eisenhower grew up
15 Symbol of sturdiness
17 High hit behind the catcher, say
18 Do surgery (on)
19 End of a school Web address
20 Salves
22 "My life ___ open book"
23 Ward off
26 Safety item for a tightrope walker
27 Pep rally shout
28 Refused
30 Tallied up
33 Neurologist or orthopedist
36 Graceful swimmer
38 Nuptial agreement
39 Spotty
41 Tidy savings
43 Miss. neighbor
44 ___ of Man
46 Paths from here to there
47 Stretchy fabric
49 Self-assurance
51 Family
52 Vegetable that rolls
53 Looks to be
57 Treble's counterpart
59 Thorny parts of roses
61 III + IV
62 Miss terribly
64 Theory of the universe, or a hint to the starts of 17-Across and 7-, 10-, 35- and 40-Down
67 Scene at a natural history museum
68 Observed secretly
69 Summer hrs. in D.C.
70 One doing leg. work
71 Derisive looks

DOWN

1 Post or Trib
2 Residence
3 Shred
4 Aide to Santa
5 Old auto inits.
6 Rebuff
7 Prosperous place
8 Kennel cries
9 ___ out (barely make)
10 Extreme effort at weight loss
11 Alpha, ___, gamma
12 Glimpsed
14 Twisty-horned antelope
16 Musical chord
21 Eye part
24 "Cómo ___ usted?"
25 Vientiane native
27 Abductors' demands
29 Eye part
31 Periphery
32 Lady and the Tramp, e.g.
33 Start a card game
34 Air France destination
35 Skilled marksman
37 Aviation-related prefix
40 Baloney
42 Inside of a paper towel roll
45 Sporting sword
48 One heeding the alarm clock
50 Symbols of meekness
54 Dodge
55 Petty
56 + and −
57 Ordered
58 Carbolic ___
59 A few
60 Nurses a drink
63 Lead-in to fetched or sighted
65 Card game with knocking
66 Spelling competition

by Lynn Lempel

16

ACROSS

1 Bay State sch.
6 Juicy fruits
11 Target of many a boxing blow
14 Sophomore's grade
15 Old Testament prophet
16 "It's no ___!"
17 Good sign on a highway
19 Reverse of NNW
20 Dollar or Budget competitor
21 Like the season before Easter
23 Floated gently in the air
26 7 on a grandfather clock
28 Prefix with potent
29 Use a rasp on
30 Comment on, as in a margin
32 Expected
33 Org. for the humane treatment of pets
35 Bobby of the N.H.L.
36 Alcoholics Anonymous has 12 of them
39 Once around a track
40 Catnip and fennel
43 Safe box opener
44 White ___ (termites)
46 Cousin of a Keogh, briefly
47 Arizona's Petrified Forest dates from this period
50 Optimistic
53 Sups
54 "___ luck?"
55 Heavy hammer
56 Bear witness
58 Consequently
59 Fr. holy woman

60 Good sign on a candy box
66 Dark time, in poetry
67 Vice President Burr
68 Weights abroad, informally
69 Scores in the end zone, for short
70 Velocity
71 Appears

DOWN

1 Western tribe
2 "___ in Black," Will Smith film
3 &
4 Layers
5 Acted rudely while in a line, maybe
6 Academics' degrees

7 High's opposite
8 Grp. that entertains the troops
9 Magician in Arthurian legend
10 Hot Japanese drink
11 Good sign on a car trunk
12 Concurrence
13 Ineffectual one, slangily
18 Helpers
22 ___ Dame
23 Bankrolls
24 Be next to
25 Good sign on a lawn
26 Good sign at a motel
27 Not well-put
31 "That feels gooood!"

34 "Above the fruited ___"
37 Kind of porridge
38 The "S" in CBS: Abbr.
41 Boast
42 Fill the stomach of
45 Dish often served with 10-Down
47 Group of cups and saucers
48 Squealed (on)
49 Despotic ruler
51 Sets (down)
52 Nickname for Elizabeth
57 Places to be pampered
58 Manage, as a bar
61 Anger
62 Actress Caldwell
63 ___ de France
64 Suffix with official
65 Twisty curve

by Robert Dillman

ACROSS

1 Lascivious
5 Dopey or Doc
10 Say jokingly
14 Zone
15 More unusual
16 Great Salt Lake's state
17 Triumph, but just barely
19 Hawaiian island
20 Badminton court divider
21 Actor Ed of "Daniel Boone"
22 Declining in power
24 False fronts
27 God, to Muslims
28 Smug smiles
30 TV, slangily, with "the"
32 Legal wrong
33 Find a new purpose for
35 Org. with admirals
38 Fall off a beam, e.g.
42 Baseballer Mel
43 Ice cream holders
44 Fusses
45 Politico Gingrich
46 Marks that look like inverted v's
48 Pago Pago's locale
51 Less drunk
54 Graduates
56 Opposite of an intro, musically
57 Parisian yes
60 MasterCard rival
61 Momentarily forget (or get lucky in Scrabble?)
64 Barely earned, with "out"
65 Ship from the Mideast
66 Suffix meaning "little"
67 M&M's that were removed from 1976 to 1987 out of a health concern for a coloring dye

68 A ton
69 Command to a steed

DOWN

1 Home turf?
2 Shallowest Great Lake
3 Led off
4 Amount of hair cream
5 All soap operas, basically
6 Declined in power
7 Got up
8 Thing, in legal briefs
9 Unoccupied, as a theater seat
10 Popular newspaper puzzle subtitled "That Scrambled Word Game"
11 Online commerce
12 Finnish bath
13 Chicken piece

18 Talk idly
23 Biblical tower site
25 Comic Johnson
26 Cigar ends
28 Capital of Manche, France
29 No longer worth debating
31 "The Star-Spangled Banner" land
33 Leases
34 WNW's opposite
35 Sworn to tell the truth
36 Glaswegian, e.g.
37 Loch ___ monster
39 Atlantic or Pacific
40 At this moment
41 Swiss river
45 Wanderers
46 Trees whose wood is used for chests
47 United ___ Emirates

48 Lifeguard, at times
49 Similar
50 Meditated (on)
52 City between Gainesville and Orlando
53 Took a curtain call
55 Fox hit "American ___"
58 "Render therefore ___ Caesar . . ."
59 Scandinavian furniture giant
62 ___ de Janeiro
63 Actor Ayres

by Andrea Carla Michaels

ACROSS

1 Baby's first word, in Italy
6 Commercials
9 Touches
14 Skip ___ (lose tempo)
15 Tennis do-over
16 Katmandu's land
17 ___ firma
18 Mai ___ (tropical drink)
19 "Yum!"
20 "Future Shock" author
23 Prefix with -lithic
24 Wetland
25 Antique restorer's efforts, for short
28 Late hunter of Nazi war criminals
34 Comedian Philips
35 Aria singer
36 Brewing coffee produces one
37 Designer Christian
39 Semesters
42 Muslim holy man
43 Shake hands (on)
45 Former senator Trent
47 ___ dye (chemical coloring)
48 "Sister Carrie" author
52 Airport schedule abbr.
53 The 1919 Treaty of Versailles concluded it: Abbr.
54 Directional suffix
55 Singing group suggested by the starts of 20-, 28- and 48-Across
61 Dragon Ball Z game company
64 ___ Solo of "Star Wars"

65 Actress Papas or Ryan
66 Thesaurus author
67 Superlative suffix
68 Girlish laugh
69 Bullwinkle, for one
70 Letter between pi and sigma
71 Actress Falco and namesakes

DOWN

1 ___ Hari
2 Brother of Cain and Seth
3 "___ Griffin's Crosswords"
4 Dolphins QB Dan
5 Finished
6 Choir voice
7 Like most users of sign language
8 Cadavers, slangily

9 Insect or radio part
10 Yogi, for one
11 FedEx competitor
12 Tit for ___
13 Crafty
21 Namely
22 Former auto executive Iacocca
25 Clarence of the Supreme Court
26 Kind of class for expectant mothers
27 Noisy shouting
28 Anesthetize, say
29 "Put me down as a maybe"
30 Tied down, as a boat
31 "___ changed my mind"
32 Country rocker Steve

33 Prefix with lateral
38 Old Olds car
40 "The ___ Squad" of '60s–'70s TV
41 Throat problem
44 First American to walk in space
46 Orkin target
49 Be in the red
50 Wealthier
51 Accustomed
55 ___ chic
56 Corned beef concoction
57 Absorbed by
58 Soda pop brand
59 Thigh/shin connector
60 Understands
61 Slot machine part
62 Excessively
63 In the past

by Michael Blake

ACROSS

1 Mrs. Dithers of the comics
5 Holder of billiard balls
9 County, in Britain
14 Breakfast chain
15 Jazz's Fitzgerald
16 Blender setting
17 Huge
18 Numbskull
19 Modern missive
20 Anger
21 Carnival treat
23 More shrewd
25 "It's not easy ___ green"
26 Like some modern music
29 ___ Pieces
33 Lindbergh's trans-Atlantic destination
35 Farm billies
37 Charlottesville sch.
38 Cutlass, e.g., informally
39 Starts of 21- and 53-Across and 3- and 30-Down
40 Gets older
41 Golf ball position
42 Storms
43 Eurasian mountains
44 The Jayhawks of the Big 12
46 Groove-making tool
48 Tiny hill dwellers
50 Skip
53 Carbonated citrus-flavored drink
58 Medical care grp.
59 Cape ___ Islands
60 Diaper problem
61 Keep ___ on (watch)
62 ___ tube
63 Nabisco best-seller
64 160 square rods
65 Jim Morrison's group, with "the"
66 Feathered missile
67 "Sure, go ahead"

DOWN

1 ___ center
2 "Gone With the Wind" surname
3 White House setting
4 Likely
5 Like many evangelicals
6 Loads
7 Arterial blockage
8 Shish ___
9 Canis lupus familiaris, for dogs
10 Compassionate
11 Neighbor of Pakistan
12 Actor/director Tim
13 Slithery
21 Corporate V.I.P.'s
22 "Phooey!"
24 "How sweet ___!"
27 Wide-eyed
28 Toward the bottom
30 1963 #1 hit for the Fireballs
31 Daredevil Knievel
32 Impudent talk
33 President before Taylor
34 Inter ___
36 Too
39 Moisten, as poultry
40 Mars' Greek counterpart
42 New York N.H.L.'ers
43 Great Salt Lake's state
45 Wood-smoothing tool
47 Result
49 Atlantic food fish
51 Shadow
52 Actress Parker ___
53 "Metamorphoses" poet
54 Nevada city
55 River through Florence
56 ___ avis
57 One getting a manual
61 Confucian path

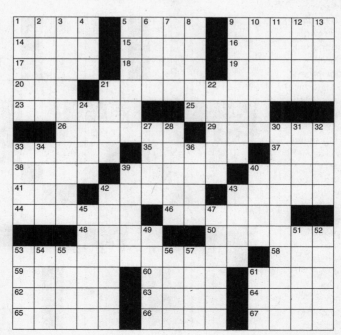

by Randy Sowell

ACROSS

1 Heartbeat
6 Impersonator in "Little Red Riding Hood"
10 Heavy, durable furniture wood
14 Santa ___ racetrack
15 Jai ___
16 Folkie Guthrie
17 Think tank products
18 Not so much
19 Dec. 25
20 Skeptic
23 Web address ender
24 "Little" girl of "Uncle Tom's Cabin"
25 What a 20-Across might say
32 Washed (down), as a sidewalk
34 Just managed, with "out"
35 Historic time
36 Cut ___ (dance)
37 Ways
39 Nose-in-the-air type
40 Snoring sound
41 Plain crazy
42 Scalds, e.g.
43 What a 20-Across might say
47 Baseball stat
48 Hoopsters' org.
49 What a 20-Across might say, ignoring grammar
57 Tobacco plug
58 Jacob's twin
59 Designer Donna
60 Wintry

61 Angry outburst
62 Turn inside out
63 Meowers
64 Bend in the wind
65 50 minutes after the hour

DOWN

1 Settled up
2 Nullify
3 Stead
4 Knife
5 Where Cockney is spoken in London
6 Heavy, durable furniture wood
7 Designer Cassini
8 Bringing up the rear
9 Unfriendly looks
10 I.R.S. worker
11 Humorist Bombeck

12 "Oh, woe!"
13 Some boxing wins, briefly
21 Wedding words
22 "Ars Amatoria" poet
25 Maker of the Rodeo
26 Computer storage unit, informally
27 Words before roses or lettuce
28 Instrument making HI notes?
29 Variety
30 Do post-laundry work
31 Setters of indents
32 Having a bit of smog
33 Ricelike pasta
37 Nicknames

38 Columbus Day's mo.
39 1 + 2 + 3, e.g.
41 Pharmaceutical workplaces
42 Relative of a quilt
44 After-Christmas shopping scenes
45 Working, as a police officer
46 Sash in Sapporo
49 "Stop!"
50 "Stop!"
51 "The Last Time ___ Paris"
52 Comic Carvey
53 "I ___ at the office"
54 Wee warbler
55 Male deer
56 Not duped by
57 Roman 300

by Harriet Clifton

ACROSS

1 Church recess
5 Wallop in the boxing ring
9 Catcher's position
14 Deception
15 "Movin' ___" ("The Jeffersons" theme song)
16 What marks and francs have been replaced with
17 Singer Braxton
18 Cunningness
19 German word of appreciation
20 Special occasion
23 Atty.'s org.
24 ___ constrictor
25 Arctic bird
26 Oz musical, with "The"
29 Beatles movie
33 State Farm's business: Abbr.
34 Cry loudly
35 E.T. transporters
36 Bank contents
39 Unilever soap brand
40 Film critic Roger
41 Wide-eyed
42 ___ Lingus
43 Roman 111
44 Winner of the first Super Bowl
50 Sushi fish
51 Dadaist Jean
52 Motorist's way: Abbr.
53 "Shucks!"
54 Where to find the colors in this puzzle
57 Gather, logically
60 Home of Città del Vaticano

61 Fit of temper
62 Capital of Ecuador
63 Spoken
64 Raced (through)
65 Cast about
66 Nerve
67 S-shaped molding

DOWN

1 Off course
2 One of the friends on "Friends"
3 Beach footwear
4 1928 Oscar winner Jannings
5 Acts obsequiously
6 Singer Bryant and others
7 Christmastime
8 Area from which to hear an aria

9 Pop crooner Neil
10 Waterfront site
11 Vase
12 "Thumbs up"
13 Mao ___-tung
21 Piano key wood
22 Boneheaded
26 Bride, after the vows
27 "Are you ___ out?"
28 Spiciness
30 Feudal lord
31 Unconscionably high interest
32 Hungarian cube maker
36 Caster of spells
37 Fairy-tale meanie
38 Christmas song
39 Spring game?
40 Do well (at)

42 Start of a magician's cry
43 Raspberry
45 Not wide
46 First
47 Holiday quaff
48 Put on the payroll again
49 Parlor piece
54 French head
55 "___ good time, call . . ."
56 "That's all there ___ it!"
57 Figs. averaging 100
58 Macadamia, e.g.
59 Spruce relative

by David Pringle

22

ACROSS

1 Poppycock
4 Explorer ___ Polo
9 God of love
13 Daredevil Knievel
15 Reside
16 Himalayan priest
17 Road sign #1
19 Genesis garden
20 Actress Verdugo of "Marcus Welby, M.D."
21 Renter's agreement
23 Item scrambled or poached
24 Will's subject
26 Road sign #2
28 Santa's helper
30 "___ harm" (medical maxim)
31 Road sign #3
37 M-1's and AK-47's
40 Slender nails
41 Life story, in brief
42 "The stage ___"
43 Child's request
44 Road sign #4
46 Oolong and others
49 Racehorse, to a bettor
50 Road sign #5
54 Wood nymphs, in myth
59 Stately tree
60 Bogged down
62 Really love something, with "up"
63 Willowy
65 Road sign #6
67 Proctor's call
68 Snakes in the road?
69 Prefix with byte
70 Observed

71 Songstress Della
72 Whom you might see in your rearview mirror if you ignore the above signs

DOWN

1 Gen. in the Confederacy
2 Flattened circles
3 Doctrine
4 Roman 1,550
5 Wanted soldier
6 Stitch again
7 Cloudless
8 Fatherland, affectionately
9 Hearty brew
10 Degraded
11 Alpha's opposite
12 Slender and long-limbed

14 Horne of "The Lady and Her Music"
18 Takes care of the food for the party
22 Musician Brian
25 Lodge member
27 Grind, as teeth
29 Little lies
31 "Peacock" network
32 ". . . man ___ mouse?"
33 Show silently
34 Fancy goodbye
35 Tiny criticism
36 Thug
38 ___ culpa
39 Regulation: Abbr.
42 "Amen!"
45 Cushion

47 Supplier of PIN money?
48 Fast pitch with a curve
50 Homes in trees
51 Kukla, Fran and ___
52 Jagged, as a leaf's edge
53 All keyed up
55 Yin's opposite
56 Cellar's opposite
57 San ___, Calif.
58 Rein, e.g.
61 Fawns' mothers
64 Fraternity members
66 Mao ___-tung

by C. W. Stewart

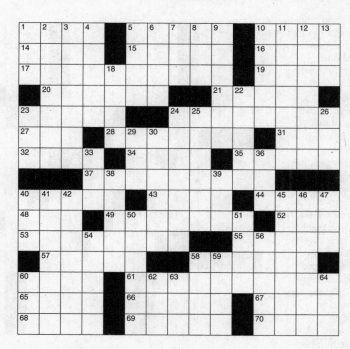

ACROSS

1 Member of a pesky swarm
5 Brighton baby buggies
10 Blighted urban area
14 Change the décor of
15 Wash gently against, as the shore
16 Camp shelter
17 Popular grilled fish
19 ___ Elevator Company
20 Not half bad
21 Concerning
23 Jordanian cash
24 Soft drink since 1885
27 Brit. reference work
28 China, Japan, etc.
31 ". . . man ___ mouse?"
32 Pâté de foie ___
34 Guns, as an engine
35 All wound up
37 1940 Ronald Reagan role
40 "Cheers" waitress
43 On the bounding main
44 "National Velvet" author Bagnold
48 Golf rarity
49 Sicilian seaport
52 Language suffix
53 Charlie Parker or Dizzy Gillespie
55 Car antitheft device
57 City trashed by Rodan
58 African desert
60 Big bash
61 Da Vinci masterpiece, with "The"

65 A.B.A. member: Abbr.
66 Started a cigarette
67 Clearance event
68 Soldiers' meal
69 Signs of things to come
70 ___ the Red

DOWN

1 Cur's warning
2 More impoverished
3 Tack-ons
4 Puccini opera
5 Course of action
6 Totally absorbed
7 PC program, briefly
8 Al Capp's Daisy ___
9 Harness parts
10 Place to sit streetside
11 Take some pressure off
12 Opposite of dividers
13 Appalachians, e.g.: Abbr.
18 Soft ball material
22 Midler of "The Rose"
23 Husky or hound
24 Inventor
25 Speaker with a sore throat, say
26 Actress ___ Dawn Chong
29 "___ we there yet?"
30 Amuse, as with anecdotes
33 Cardinal's insignia
36 Poet's before
38 All smiles
39 Antistick cooking spray
40 Part of a semi
41 Overlay material

42 Makes tighter, in a way
45 Close to its face value, as a bond
46 Ehud Barak or Ehud Olmert
47 Nancy Pelosi, e.g.: Abbr.
50 Moon-landing program
51 Pearl Harbor's site
54 Gives the go-ahead
56 Run out, as a subscription
58 Zap with a Taser
59 Nile slitherers
60 Pinup's leg
62 Align the cross hairs
63 Sault ___ Marie
64 ___ room (play area)

by Fred Piscop

ACROSS

1 1960s–'70s draft org.
4 Purse feature
9 Where hair roots grow
14 Photo
15 Singers Ochs and Collins
16 Causing goosebumps
17 Excitement
18 Pulitzer-winning biography of a Civil War general
19 Take in or let out
20 Modern fashion-conscious guys
23 Didn't participate in
24 Circular staples
25 Appropriate
28 Use a swizzle stick
30 Reception amenity
33 Clubs or hearts
36 Central point
38 Shinbone
39 Unlikely showing at a multiplex
43 Germ cell
44 Day-___ paint
45 "___ of the D'Urbervilles"
46 Item on a gunslinger's hip
49 Bangkok native
51 Perry Como's "___ Impossible"
52 Nectar collector
54 List at a meeting
58 Yanks vs. Mets matchup, e.g.
61 Olympics craft
64 "You ___ right!"
65 ___ Lilly and Company
66 Delight
67 Suddenly cut out, as an engine
68 Rogue
69 Nintendo products
70 Sprayed, as a sidewalk
71 Iris's place

DOWN

1 Sends unwanted e-mails
2 Most-played half of a 45
3 Willard of "Today"
4 Bamboo beginning
5 1973 Newman/Redford movie
6 Annoy
7 Billy Joel's musical daughter
8 Prefix with intellectual
9 Circus performer with a ball
10 Disney collectibles
11 Paintings
12 Fail a polygraph
13 The "p" in r.p.m.
21 Lists
22 Dangerous hisser
25 Hoffman of 1960s–'70s radicalism
26 Buckets
27 Mine transports
29 Karel Capek classic
31 LAX posting
32 Cooler
33 Some Japanese cuisine
34 Prepare to transplant
35 Fan mail recipients
37 Morass
40 No longer working: Abbr.
41 Final: Abbr.
42 Easy, as a loan
47 Recede
48 Clean again
50 Ancient
53 Keep an ___ the ground
55 Nephew's sister
56 Holdup
57 In reserve
58 Fill up
59 Hawaiian strings, informally
60 "Pro" votes
61 Beer bust purchase
62 Like
63 Thanksgiving side dish

by Joy C. Frank

ACROSS

1 "My Fair Lady" horse race
6 Wrigley Field team
10 Hinged fastener
14 Tiresome task
15 "Got it"
16 Germany's von Bismarck
17 Film director Frank
18 Sharp-toothed Atlantic swimmer
20 Ron of Tarzan fame
21 Record-setting miler Sebastian
23 Diner's bill
24 Actress Gardner
25 Overabundance
28 Washing site
30 Fuss
31 Toyota rival
34 Must-have
35 Holey cheese
37 Entice
39 Doohickey
43 Sir ___ Newton
44 Skin woes
47 Total flop
50 Evening up, as a score
53 Ice cream purchase
54 About 71% of the earth's surface
56 All-time winningest N.F.L. coach
58 The "I" in T.G.I.F.
59 Acorn producer
62 ___ and Coke
63 Seize
64 1978 Donna Summer hit . . . or a hint to 18-, 25-, 39- and 56-Across
67 Tennis's Agassi

69 Nights before holidays
70 Wines like Merlot
71 Prolonged attack
72 Office furniture
73 Annoyer
74 Jackrabbits, actually

DOWN

1 Takes, as an offer
2 Not deep
3 Tweak, as magazine text
4 Hockey legend Bobby
5 Class instructor, informally
6 Roman orator
7 Grp. putting on shows for troops
8 Not straight

9 Big video game maker
10 Opposite of vert.
11 Relaxed
12 Musical Wonder
13 Pope John Paul II's homeland
19 Diminish
22 Cry of wonder
26 Tokyo electronics giant
27 Heartburn reliever
29 Ohio college named for a biblical city
32 Rep.'s foe
33 Dr.'s advocate
36 Lisa, to Bart Simpson
38 Bedwear, briefly
40 ___ King Cole
41 Not straight

42 Alternative to a fly ball
45 Expand
46 Navy building crew
47 Heated, as water
48 "Do, re, mi, fa, sol, la, ti, do" range
49 Slobs' creations
51 What the weary get, in a saying
52 Horned beast
55 Silent O.K.
57 Huge hit
60 Org. for those 50+
61 Thigh/shin separator
65 "For shame!"
66 PC inserts
68 Vardalos of "My Big Fat Greek Wedding"

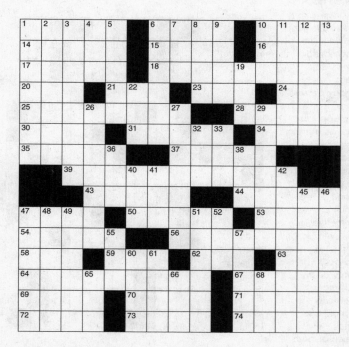

by Lynn Lempel

26

ACROSS

1 "Survivor" shelter
4 $$$ dispenser
7 Circumference
12 October birthstone
14 ___ Fox of Uncle Remus tales
16 "I love you," in Spanish
17 The year 1052
18 Be an omen of
19 Lady
20 007's introduction
23 Dustin's role in "Midnight Cowboy"
24 Sand holders at the beach
25 Slugger's stat
28 Mag. workers
29 Hip-hop doc?
31 Part of an ellipsis
32 Prominent part of a dachshund
33 Easy as ___
34 Except
35 Birthday dessert
36 Embroidered sampler phrase
40 Guns, as a motor
41 Cravat
42 Almost forever
43 Byron's "before"
44 "My gal" of song
45 Branch
46 Commercial suffix with Gator
49 Each
50 Map book
52 County on the Thames
54 Repeatedly
57 Soup eater's sound
59 Kitchen or bath
60 Aroma

61 Hearing-related
62 College digs
63 Traveled
64 Tableau
65 Airport screening org.
66 Snake's sound

DOWN

1 Man of La Mancha
2 Transfer to a mainframe, maybe
3 Contaminates
4 Alphabetically first pop group with a #1 hit
5 ___ l'oeil
6 Tragic woman in Greek drama
7 Maximally
8 Nasty
9 Nightmare

10 Britney Spears's "___ Slave 4 U"
11 Mr. Turkey
13 Jar tops
15 Ashes, e.g.
21 "Panic Room" actress Foster
22 Ink soaker-upper
26 Make a 35-Across
27 Anger
30 Say again just for the record, say
33 Afternoons, for short
34 Queen who might create quite a buzz?
35 Pro's opposite
36 Roll-call call
37 Orchestral intro
38 Weatherman Scott

39 "The Simpsons" dad
40 Agent, in brief
44 Just a taste
45 Noted family of financiers and philanthropists
46 Parenthetical comments
47 Fiends
48 Puts forth, as effort
51 In progress
53 Put away
55 Gulf land
56 Gwyneth Paltrow title role
57 Carrier to Stockholm
58 Capt. Jean-___ Picard of the U.S.S. Enterprise

by Andrea Carla Michaels

ACROSS

1 Tempest
6 Cub Scout group
9 Singer Turner and others
14 Chili con ___
15 N.Y.C.'s Park or Lexington
16 "Dying / Is ___, like anything else": Sylvia Plath
17 E. M. Forster novel
20 Brooks of comedy
21 Old punch line?
22 Disreputable
23 Mia of women's soccer
24 To ___ (perfectly)
25 Car parker
32 One of the Astaires
33 Dictionary unit
34 Australian hopper, for short
35 Manner
36 Property encumbrances
38 "Cómo ___ usted?"
39 Hosp. scan
40 Cost of a cab
41 C-3PO, for one
42 Entities cited in the Penitential Rite
46 Tipplers
47 The Vatican's home
48 "La Nausée" novelist
51 "Star Wars" guru
52 Opposite of 'neath
55 What conspiracy theorists look for (as hinted at by 17-, 25- and 42-Across)
58 Colorado ski town
59 Dined
60 Spanish hero played by Charlton Heston
61 Louts
62 "Two clubs," e.g., in bridge
63 Cuts down on calories

DOWN

1 E-mail offer of $17,000,000.00, e.g.
2 Reel-to-reel ___
3 Spoken
4 I.C.U. helpers
5 Communiqué
6 Explorer Vasco ___
7 Even once
8 Ping-Pong table divider
9 Last part
10 Wanting
11 Zilch
12 Phoenix's home: Abbr.
13 Order to Fido
18 Peak
19 Some blenders
23 Robust
24 Lots
25 Letter after beta
26 Decorate
27 Excavate again
28 11- or 12-year-old
29 Crime sometimes done for the insurance
30 Untagged, in a game
31 Creatures said to cause warts
36 Remained
37 Gershwin and others
38 Cleveland's lake
40 Old gold coins
41 Requiring repair
43 Rolle who starred in "Good Times"
44 Spoke so as to put people to sleep
45 Ice cream drink
48 Dagger wound
49 "I see," facetiously
50 "___ Man," Emilio Estevez movie
51 Dubious sighting in the Himalayas
52 A single time
53 Blue-pencil
54 X-ray units
56 Small amount, as of hair cream
57 Inventor Whitney

by Peter A. Collins

ACROSS

1 Digging tool
6 ___ McAn shoes
10 Felt remorse
14 Israel's Sharon
15 Lira's replacement
16 "Don't Tread ___" (old flag warning)
17 Planter without hired hands
19 Game-stopping call
20 "Zip-___-Doo-Dah"
21 "I didn't know that!"
22 Nervous giggle
24 Fabrics for towels, robes, etc.
26 Sukiyaki side dish
27 Auto mechanic
32 Nests, for birds
35 Fall site in Genesis
36 Eco-friendly org.
37 ___ Brothers, who sang "Rag Mop"
38 Fur tycoon John Jacob
40 Trickle out
41 A Bobbsey twin
42 Leave off
43 Storied engineer Casey
44 Any member of Nirvana or Pearl Jam
48 Java dispensers
49 Take back
53 Popular drink mix
56 Extra-wide, on a shoebox
57 Fitzgerald who knew how to scat
58 Eurasia's ___ Mountains
59 Smear campaigner
62 Race that once had a four-minute barrier
63 Give off
64 Knight's mount
65 Borscht vegetable
66 D.C. nine, for short
67 Pig voiced by Mel Blanc

DOWN

1 Begin's co-Nobelist
2 Family of lions
3 Broadcaster
4 Cleanses
5 Keebler baker, in ads
6 Humanitarian Mother ___
7 Actor Cronyn
8 Smelter input
9 Edgar Bergen dummy ___ Snerd
10 Way past ripe
11 Condo or apartment
12 Noted plus-size model
13 ___ Xing (sign)
18 "The Morning Watch" writer James
23 Clickable screen symbol
25 E-file receiver
26 Change the décor of
28 Brief tussle
29 Like an eagle's vision
30 Blunted sword
31 Big fat mouths
32 Nail to the wall
33 Epps of TV's "House"
34 Chalkboard writing at a cafe
38 Emphatic words of agreement
39 Knighted ones
40 Bay of Naples tourist city
42 Hideous sort
43 Namath, for most of his career
45 Small seed
46 Blue jay toppers
47 It runs from stem to stern
50 "Ragged Dick" writer Horatio
51 One iron, in old golf lingo
52 Late, on a report card
53 Under the effects of Novocain
54 Lake named after an Indian tribe
55 Red-tag event
56 Trim, as text
60 Actress Thurman
61 AOL, e.g.: Abbr.

by Fred Piscop

ACROSS

1 More eccentric
6 "Moby-Dick" captain
10 Reaction to a knee-slapper
14 Old pal
15 Food that may come in small cubes
16 Giant-screen film venue
17 Sign for a person in therapy?
20 ___, due, tre . . .
21 Abominable Snowman
22 Turtle's covering
23 Like college aptitude tests, for many students
26 Highway
28 Compete in a slalom
29 Moist
31 Lawyer: Abbr.
35 Together
38 "Well, then . . ."
40 By way of
41 Sign for a recovering alcoholic?
43 Annoy
44 Completely cover
46 "Hmmm . . ."
48 Japanese drink
49 Numbered hwys.
51 Faux ___
52 Perlman of "Cheers"
54 Comedian's gimmick
58 Candidate Stevenson of '52 and '56
61 Level
63 Rhetorical question, possibly
64 Sign for a gangster?
68 Fork prong
69 Washington daily
70 ___ Ste. Marie, Mich.
71 Went fast
72 Aussie jumpers
73 ___ Rose Lee

DOWN

1 Happen
2 Pilotless aircraft
3 Sign for a jury selector?
4 Suffix with differ
5 Seedy loaf
6 Eventgoer
7 Party thrower
8 Uphold
9 Prickly seed cover
10 Religious time
11 French girlfriend
12 Room connector
13 Skating jump
18 Science guy Bill
19 Cool ___ cucumber
24 Letters before an alias
25 Twists to be worked out
27 Eye-catching designs
30 Enough
32 Sign for a sunbather?
33 Went fast
34 Oxen connector
35 Currier and ___
36 Companion of the Pinta and Santa Maria
37 Plowmaker John
39 Pretty maiden of Greek myth
42 Mousse and mud pie
45 Exposed to oxygen
47 Consume
50 Skin art
53 Go quickly
55 ___-Magnon
56 They're stirred in the fire
57 Meower
58 Many urban homes: Abbr.
59 Annoyance from a faucet
60 "The ___ Ranger"
62 In that case
65 E.M.T.'s skill
66 "No ___" (Chinese menu notation)
67 It's pitched with a pitchfork

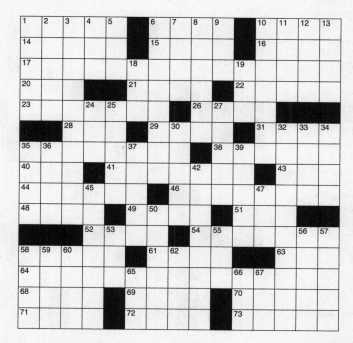

by Kevin Der

ACROSS

1 Like some committees
6 Designer Lauren
11 Lunch counter sandwich, for short
14 How most mail goes nowadays
15 Accustom to hardship
16 Whopper
17 Sinuous Mideast entertainer
19 Multivolume Brit. reference
20 Ballpark fig.
21 www addresses
22 Beaded counter
24 Basic course for a future M.D.
25 The "A" in DNA
26 Chance, at cards
31 Compass part
33 David Sedaris's comic sister
34 Springsteen's "Born in the ___"
35 Golfer Palmer, familiarly
36 Gives the green light
37 Pesto ingredient
39 Comic Caesar
40 New Year's ___
41 Yield
42 One way to fall in love
46 Goatee site
47 Blockheads
48 Dietetic
51 Novelist Ambler
52 "Without further ___ . . ."
55 ___ carte
56 Host of a Friars Club event
59 Chess pieces
60 ___ forth (et cetera)
61 Vibes

62 Word that may precede the beginning of 17-, 26-, 42- or 56-Across
63 Most common craps roll
64 Yahoo! or AOL offering

DOWN

1 French cleric
2 Colors, as Easter eggs
3 Sentry's command
4 Mideast export
5 Throw in the towel
6 Theater district
7 Raggedy ___ (dolls)
8 Film director Jean-___ Godard
9 Tediously didactic
10 Jazz's Hancock or Mann
11 Voting group
12 Stead
13 Senators Kennedy and Stevens
18 Explorer Sir Francis
23 Append
24 BMW competitor
25 Places to get quick money, quickly
26 ___ hand (help)
27 Fraud
28 Stratagems
29 Z ___ zebra
30 Poet Whitman
31 Poet Ogden
32 Shallowest of the Great Lakes

36 Pizzeria fixture
37 Muscle mag photos
38 Cure-___ (panaceas)
40 Satan, with "the"
41 Adjust one's sights
43 Roman 700
44 Tara plantation family
45 Dr. Seuss's "___ Hears a Who"
48 Genie's home
49 Butter alternative
50 Privation
51 To be, in old Rome
52 Gillette ___ Plus
53 Prefix with god
54 Said aloud
57 Really or truly, e.g.: Abbr.
58 Wal-Mart founder Walton

by Richard Chisholm

ACROSS

1 Cousins of mandolins
6 Marx with a manifesto
10 Not shallow
14 "Faust" or "Don Giovanni"
15 Hodgepodge
16 Neutral tone
17 Simple pleasure
20 Doctors' bags
21 Often-stained piece of attire
22 Manipulate
23 Drip from a pipe, e.g.
24 Leftover bit
28 Old Iran
30 Preordain
32 Daily allowance
35 Unruly head of hair
36 1978 Rolling Stones hit
40 Caribbean, e.g.
41 Worker in a stable
42 Humor that's often lost in an e-mail
45 Proverb
49 ___ B. Anthony dollar
50 Two of a kind
52 Word with neither
53 Four-alarm fire
56 Where 6-Down is
57 Sex appeal
61 Aria singer
62 ___ quilt (modern memorial)
63 Kind of pole
64 Plow pullers
65 Gait between walk and canter
66 Tickle

DOWN

1 Put in jail
2 Revolt
3 Be on the verge of falling
4 Periods in history
5 Day of the wk. . . . or an exam usually taken on that day
6 Seoul's home
7 Smart ___
8 Basketball coach Pitino
9 Stolen money
10 Flaw
11 Modern prefix with tourism
12 Blow it
13 Postpone, with "off"
18 Digs up
19 "Little ___ Sunshine"
23 Untruths
25 Coating of frost
26 In the near future
27 Get-up-and-go
29 Where you might get into hot water
30 Credit card bills, e.g.
31 Photographic film coating
33 Inevitable destruction
34 No ___, ands or buts
36 Boyfriend
37 Distinctive features of Mr. Spock
38 Backside
39 Empty, as a well
40 Radiator sound
43 Alligatorlike reptile
44 "The King and I" woman
46 Where originally found
47 Bump and thump
48 British weight
50 Home of many Velázquez paintings
51 Uneasy feeling
54 Kansaslike
55 Arab chieftain
56 ___ smasher
57 Hurly-burly
58 Veto
59 "If ___ told you once . . ."
60 When the pilot is due in, for short

by Eric Fischer

32

ACROSS

1 With 71-Across, sort of person who might enjoy this puzzle?
6 Narrow cut
10 Like show horses' feet
14 Make up (for)
15 Comfort
16 Voice quality
17 Person in a polling booth
18 Good for what ___ you
19 Not written
20 Saying about the heart
23 One of the Kennedys
24 Hot to the tongue
25 ___ Four (Beatles)
28 Shuffles off this mortal coil
31 Bad-mouth
32 Wonder
33 Sonja Henie's Norwegian birthplace
35 Clamor
39 Crazy
43 Collect
44 It can sense scents
45 Pie ___ mode
46 Size above sm.
48 Campaign pros
50 Singer Rawls or Reed
51 Was patient for
55 Suffix with meteor
57 Outcast
63 Decorate again
64 Letter-shaped girder
65 Pertaining to warships
66 TV's "American ___"
67 Demolish
68 Songstress Baker

69 Instrument that's plucked
70 Elevator pioneer Elisha
71 See 1-Across

DOWN

1 Volcanic discharge
2 Part of a molecule
3 "The Wizard of Oz" dog
4 Unmoving
5 Strengthened
6 Actor Penn
7 Secular
8 Waterfront Long Island town
9 Tried out
10 Crushes with the feet
11 Lena who sang "Stormy Weather"

12 Walking ___ (happy)
13 What rain may cause
21 Expression
22 Think out loud
25 Werewolf's tooth
26 G.I. no-show
27 The "B" of N.B.
29 Channel for armchair athletes
30 Single-masted boat
34 ___ buco
36 Leaning, as type: Abbr.
37 Building beside a barn
38 Jacob's twin in the Bible
40 Woman's sheer undergarment
41 ___ a customer

42 Cantaloupe, e.g.
47 Robert of "Raging Bull"
49 Cue
51 First full month of spring
52 Overrun with dandelions and such
53 Passion
54 Touch lightly, as the corner of one's eye
56 Popular pipe clearer
58 Ultra-authoritarian
59 Mined rocks
60 Tel ___
61 London museum
62 Wing-shaped

by Richard Hughes

ACROSS

1 Lhasa ___ (dog)
5 High Hollywood honor
10 Ice hockey venue
14 "All ___ is divided into three parts"
15 Distress signal
16 First garden
17 German auto
18 *Park ranger's worry
20 Czech or Croat
21 Speak from a soapbox
22 Lab eggs
23 *Conifer exudation
26 Hopped to it
28 Pals
29 Come in last
31 ___ Doria (ill-fated ship)
34 Vagrant
38 Gossip queen Barrett
39 Like the starts of the answers to the six starred clues
41 Supply-and-demand subj.
42 Lively horses
44 Sudden
46 Mama ___ of the Mamas and the Papas
47 Command for Rover
48 Former Iranian leaders
51 *Metaphor for dense fog
55 Kernel holder
56 Sum
60 Adjust the pitch of
61 *Large seed of the alligator pear
64 Abbr. before the name of a memo recipient
65 ___ Strauss & Co.
66 1970s music fad
67 53, in old Rome
68 Not guilty, e.g.
69 Shuteye
70 Nifty

DOWN

1 Visibly horrified
2 Sainted eighth-century pope
3 Khartoum's land
4 *Peace offering
5 Popular insect repellent
6 Sailing vessels
7 Caleb who wrote "The Alienist"
8 Length × width, for a rectangle
9 Breather
10 Ump
11 Moron
12 Chutzpah
13 Work, as dough
19 Josh
24 Seek damages from
25 Proverbs
27 *Crunchy item at a salad bar
29 Gen. Meade's foe at Gettysburg
30 Rococo
31 Dadaist Jean
32 Neither's partner
33 Crime scene evidence
34 ___ Moines
35 Post-op location
36 Badge wearer
37 Explosive inits.
40 B. & O. and Reading: Abbr.
43 Words before spell, shadow or wide net
45 Sheep's cry
47 Put together, as film
48 Where hair roots grow
49 Shack
50 Superior to
52 Certain belly button
53 Loosen, as a knot
54 Enclose, as farm animals
57 Ten to one, e.g.
58 Hard work
59 Church recess
62 Spy org.
63 Blouse or shirt

by J. K. Hummel

34

ACROSS

1 Gadabout
6 Dads' counterpart
10 Disconcert
14 January, in Juárez
15 Jai ___
16 Desertlike
17 Like folks cared for by former congressman Bob?
19 Telephone sound
20 Whichever
21 Book after Joel
22 Infuriate
24 Use a swizzle stick
25 Street urchin
26 Pollux's twin
29 Man of steel?
33 Wedding site
34 Quick job in a barbershop
35 Short-term worker
36 Max of "The Beverly Hillbillies"
37 "___ enough!"
38 Part of a judge's workload
39 Gen. Bradley
40 Sports "zebras"
41 Little Pigs' count
42 Boy genius of juvenile fiction
44 Holders of pirate treasures
45 Sword handle
46 Not single-sex, as a school
47 Naval affirmative
50 Complete flop
51 "Steady as ___ goes"
54 Angel's instrument
55 Like funds gathered by singer Vikki?
58 Writer Wiesel
59 Math class, in brief
60 Trap
61 Patch up

62 When Romeo meets Juliet
63 Dwarfs' count

DOWN

1 McEntire of country and western
2 ___ even keel
3 Extremely
4 Do something boneheaded
5 The spit in a spit roast, e.g.
6 Country estate
7 Bygone G.M. make
8 Screen siren West
9 Pistols and such
10 Like a ball retrieved by actor Jamie?
11 Diva's delivery

12 Get but good
13 Upper hand
18 Kuwaiti leader
23 "Delta of Venus" writer Anaïs
24 Like clay molded by drummer Ringo?
25 Does a garçon's job
26 Explorer Sebastian
27 Texas battle site of 1836
28 Geyser's emission
29 Knitting or beadwork
30 First, second, third and reverse
31 "No more, thanks"
32 Sporting blades

34 Larceny
37 Racetrack bet
41 Springsteen, to fans
43 Modus operandi
44 Freebie
46 Welsh dog
47 "Uh . . . excuse me"
48 Ivy League school
49 Land of leprechauns
50 Londoner or Liverpudlian, e.g.
51 Eastern European
52 "Kilroy was ___"
53 Genesis garden
56 Path of a javelin
57 White Monopoly bill

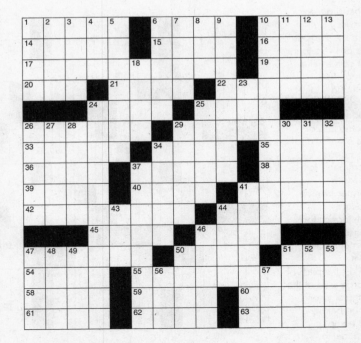

by Randall J. Hartman

ACROSS

1 Like some 1930s design, informally
5 Mafia biggie
9 Light from a lightning bug, e.g.
13 ___ Gay (W.W. II plane)
15 Worm's place on a fishing line
16 Make over
17 3"×5" aids for speakers
19 Out of control
20 Take to court
21 Formerly, old-style
22 Sky-blue
23 Corporate office staffers
27 WNW's opposite
28 Elevator company
29 Shut loudly
32 Des Moines native
34 E.T.'s craft
37 Identify exactly . . . or a hint to this puzzle's theme
41 Lumberjacking tool
42 Edgar ___ Poe
43 It might be slapped after a good joke
44 Writer ___ Stanley Gardner
45 New Year's ___
47 Fonzie's girl on "Happy Days"
54 Surrenders
55 Leo's symbol
56 Ph.D., e.g.: Abbr.
57 End-___ (ultimate buyer)
58 Head of a cabal
61 Doe's mate
62 Tehran's land
63 Add liquor to, as punch
64 Roly-___
65 Mishmash
66 "___ of the D'Urbervilles"

DOWN

1 Basic religious belief
2 Boredom
3 In secret language
4 Encouragement for a matador
5 Deep gap
6 Main artery
7 Pea holder
8 10-4's
9 Barely injures in passing
10 Cousin of a monkey
11 Stinks
12 Regained consciousness
14 Figure skating jumps
18 Indian of the northern Plains
22 Getting on in years
24 Record sent to a record producer
25 Hopeless, as a situation
26 ___ all-time high
29 Site of mineral waters
30 Illumination unit
31 Dined
32 Bit of land in the sea
33 Birds ___ feather
34 Vase
35 Enemy
36 Last number in a countdown
38 Drug agents: Var.
39 ___ May of "The Beverly Hillbillies"
40 Scraped (out)
44 Cabinet department since 1977
45 E.P.A. subj.
46 Barn toppers
47 Sauce in un ristorante
48 Perfect
49 Arm bones
50 Omens
51 Murphy who's heard in "Shrek"
52 Stinks
53 Meanies
54 Edge
58 Edge
59 Wrath
60 Fitting

by David Pringle

36

ACROSS

1 King Kong's kin
5 Dry out
10 Aspen gear
14 N.Y.C. cultural center
15 Big name in can-making
16 Tight curl
17 Elastic holder
19 Opposed to
20 Depart's opposite
21 Lisa, to Bart
23 Actor Beatty
24 "Cheers" woman
25 Home of Notre Dame
28 Abbr. at the end of a company's name
29 1986 Indy 500 winner Bobby
31 Clear, as a chalkboard
32 S-shaped molding
34 Three Stooges laugh
35 Dreaded
36 Entrance, as through oratory
39 Macaroni and manicotti
42 Landon who ran for president in 1936
43 1978 hit with the lyric "You can get yourself clean, you can have a good meal"
47 Non-earthling
48 Win the first four games in a World Series, e.g.
50 Gear part
51 Ian Fleming creation
53 "Filthy" money
55 Stereo component
56 Deviation in a rocket's course

57 Actor Brando
58 Miniature plateau
60 1930s political group
63 Bustles
64 Filmmaker Coen
65 Neighborhood
66 Lost seaworthiness
67 Eccentric
68 Separators on badminton courts

DOWN

1 Medium for mostly news and talk these days
2 Raining cats and dogs
3 Hug
4 Polio vaccine developer
5 Whittle down
6 Priest's vestment
7 Color TV pioneer
8 Certain diplomat
9 "I've ___!" (cry of impatience)
10 Jamaican music
11 Greg of "You've Got Mail"
12 Strong, as emotions
13 Lost control of a car, say
18 At any time
22 Luster
25 Synagogue
26 Chicago suburb
27 Two-time Super Bowl M.V.P. Tom
30 Affirmative votes
33 ___ Lauder cosmetics
35 Flute in a march
37 Variety of violet

38 Ran in the wash
39 Nightclothes
40 Oakland's county
41 Bart or Lisa
44 Doug of "The Virginian"
45 Royal headgear
46 Lists for meetings
48 Part of Johannesburg
49 Schedule
52 Item on which to put lox
54 City-related
57 Quite a few
59 Query
61 Letter between pi and sigma
62 Rand McNally product

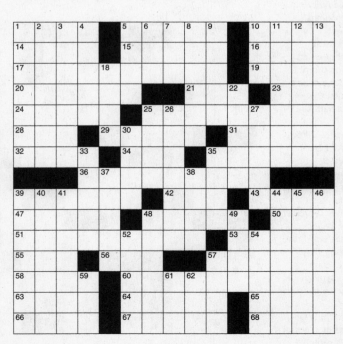

by Allan E. Parrish

ACROSS

1 Base on balls
5 Lowly chess piece
9 Afro-Brazilian dance
14 Nastase of tennis
15 Feel sore
16 "___ Gold" (1997 film)
17 See 18-Across
18 Grand ___ (annual French auto 17-Across)
19 "Carmen" composer
20 "The Breakfast Club" actor
23 Preceder of com or org
24 Desperately needing a map
25 Dangerous person
28 Donkey
29 Officer's honorific
30 '60s war site
31 More work than required
36 Lyricist Gershwin
37 "Um, excuse me"
38 "Foucault's Pendulum" author
39 The "A" in ABM
40 "My mama done ___ me"
41 It may come as a shock to a diver
45 Put to a purpose
46 Accomplished
47 French vacation time
48 Argentine grassland
50 Be wide-open
52 Salary
55 Domain ruled from Constantinople
58 Actor John of "The Addams Family"
60 ___ California
61 Pastel shade

62 Michaels of "S.N.L."
63 Brilliant display
64 Bath fixtures
65 Philadelphia N.H.L.er
66 Burden of proof
67 Radiator output

DOWN

1 Sent by telegraph
2 1836 battle site
3 Permissible
4 Part of a hull
5 Native American baby
6 Farm units
7 Early form of bridge
8 Cry at a motor vehicle bureau
9 Undermine
10 Green card holder
11 Floor between first and second
12 Spell-off
13 Winter hrs. in Bermuda
21 Ingrid's role in "Casablanca"
22 Ruler of Qatar
26 ___ blanche
27 Communication that may have an attachment
28 Sleeve filler
29 Chimney sweep's target
31 Devour hungrily
32 South African native
33 Rocket data
34 Nourish
35 TV watchdog: Abbr.

39 Good card to have "in the hole"
41 Lou Grant portrayer
42 Santa checks his twice, in song
43 Second airings
44 Topic of gossip
49 Thomas who wrote "Common Sense"
50 Corn or oat
51 Pear variety
52 Tickle, as one's interest
53 Dutch-speaking Caribbean island
54 It makes dough rise
56 Spanish river to the Mediterranean
57 ___ Trail
58 TV extraterrestrial
59 Note between fa and la

by Janet Bender

38

ACROSS

1 Some Apple computers
6 Fall behind
9 Milan's La ___
14 End of an Aesop fable
15 Eggs
16 Secret languages
17 *Mock rock band in a 1984 film
19 From the country
20 Hides the gray
21 Old-fashioned "Scram!"
22 "Dear" dispenser of advice
25 *Revealer of vowels, on TV
28 Hardly trim
30 Enclosure for grain or coal
31 "Cut it out!"
32 Hearing-related
33 Hawaiian veranda
35 *Part of a Valentine's Day bouquet
37 *Seasoned seaman
42 The mating game?
44 Rarin' to go
45 Citrus coolers
49 Parts of lbs.
50 Tie the knot
51 *Local place for making deposits or getting loans
54 ___ empty stomach
55 Garb
56 Long, long time
58 Around, as a year
59 Be logical . . . or what the last words of the answers to the five starred clues can do?
64 Parts of eyes
65 Nothing's opposite
66 Rub out
67 Oozes
68 "Affirmative"
69 Pub projectiles

DOWN

1 Quick online notes, for short
2 Clean the floor
3 ___ Onassis, Jackie Kennedy's #2
4 Butterfinger or 3 Musketeers
5 Smite
6 "___ luck!"
7 Gardner of "The Night of the Iguana"
8 Space between the teeth, e.g.
9 Fastener that turns
10 Robitussin suppresses them
11 Skillful
12 Crude shelter
13 Dozing
18 Impose, as a tax
21 Yawn-inspiring
22 From quite a distance
23 Azure
24 Poet
26 Org. with a 24-second shot clock
27 Bogotá boys
29 Voting coalition
33 Talk show host Gibbons
34 Notion
36 Ocean's edge
38 Tokyo "ta-ta!"
39 Not fer
40 Mother of Helen, in myth
41 1982 sci-fi film
43 Tax ID
45 You can always count on this
46 Latin case
47 Course before dessert
48 Headwear on the slopes
50 Place for a lawn mower
52 Military bigwigs
53 Phones
57 Was in debt
59 Stable diet?
60 Cheer for a matador
61 Road surface
62 Ballpark fig.
63 High-___ monitor

by Paula Gamache

ACROSS

1 Late bridge columnist Truscott
5 Cry made with a flourish
9 ___ Park, Colo.
14 Of sound mind
15 Cheers for toreros
16 Seismic occurrence
17 Supreme Court justice known for a literalist interpretation of the Bill of Rights
19 Earthy pigment
20 Flub
21 Employee cards with photos, e.g.
22 Squad with red, white and blue uniforms
24 Deny
26 Three-card ___
27 Public square
29 Infer (from)
33 Analyze, as ore
36 Perry Mason's creator ___ Stanley Gardner
38 Eurasian duck
39 Cut, as a lawn
40 Los Angeles N.B.A.er
41 Yellowfin, e.g.
42 Jai ___
43 "Break ___!" ("Good luck!")
44 Violin bow application
45 Thrill-seeker's watercraft
47 Subject
49 Tom who played Forrest Gump
51 Former mayor who wrote "Mayor"
55 Emancipate
58 Show the effect of weight
59 Syllable repeated after "hot"
60 Napoleon on St. Helena, e.g.
61 Pie filling

64 Fracas
65 Winnie-the-___
66 Auto racer Yarborough
67 Religion of the Koran
68 Popular frozen dessert chain
69 Signs, as a contract

DOWN

1 Pale-faced
2 First lady after Hillary
3 Red-faced, maybe
4 Prefix with conservative
5 "What'd I say?!"
6 "___, poor Yorick! I knew him, Horatio"
7 Follower of Nov.
8 Provide an invitation for

9 Consider identical
10 Some theater productions
11 Perfume brand
12 Barely makes, with "out"
13 Antitoxins
18 Onion-flavored roll
23 Follower of rear or week
25 1966 Herb Alpert & the Tijuana Brass hit
26 What the last words of 17- and 61-Across and 10- and 25-Down are kinds of
28 Ardor
30 Don of morning radio
31 "___, vidi, vici"
32 Actor McGregor
33 Key related to F# minor: Abbr.

34 Only
35 Go for, as a fly
37 Toy block brand
40 Frankie who sang "Mule Train"
44 Chain of hills
46 Hoops great Abdul-Jabbar
48 A-O.K.
50 Well-groomed
52 Surfing spot
53 Writer on a slate
54 Loathes
55 Vehicle that can jackknife
56 Alimony receivers, e.g.
57 Cash register
58 Look-down-one's-nose type
62 Quadrennial games grp.
63 Sprint rival, once

by Allan E. Parrish

40

ACROSS

1 Penny-pinch
6 Woes
10 Oats, to Trigger
14 "Deck the Halls," e.g.
15 Belle's gent
16 Auto shaft
17 Sex appeal
20 ___ judicata
21 Vintner's container
22 Some coffee orders
23 Amateur radioer
24 Initiation, e.g.
25 Where to grow carrots and spinach
33 Lycée, par exemple
34 Two cubed
35 Tool that's swung
36 It's typical
37 Anchor hoister
38 Scratch on a gem, e.g.
39 Bullring cheer
40 "Don't let these guys escape!"
41 Flinch or blink, say
42 Places to find some gems
45 "___ in China"
46 D-Day craft: Abbr.
47 Briny
50 & 52 Thomas Gainsborough portrait, with "The"
55 Game suggested by the first words of 17-, 25- and 42-Across
58 Super-duper
59 Continental coin
60 Go over, as lines

61 Latch (onto)
62 Aries or Libra
63 Flower with rays

DOWN

1 Memento of a knife fight
2 "Citizen ___"
3 Rainbow goddess
4 Soccer ___
5 Appease
6 Some early PC's
7 Unauthorized disclosure
8 Not keep up
9 Source of vitamin D
10 Not so slim
11 Sartre's "No ___"
12 If not
13 Clinton followers, for short

18 See 30-Down
19 Really bug
23 Place for a captain
24 Government in power
25 What a fang ejects
26 Worrisome food contamination
27 Charles who wrote "Winning Bridge Made Easy"
28 John, Paul, George or Ringo
29 Resided
30 With 18-Down, Tibetan V.I.P.
31 Meticulous
32 Brilliantly colored salamanders

37 Sharpshooters
38 Suffix with gab or song
40 Research money
41 ___ Stone (hieroglyphic key)
43 Rapper aka Slim Shady
44 +
47 Men-only
48 Way off base?
49 Jay who does "Jaywalking"
50 One-horse town
51 Ponce de ___
52 Ferry or dinghy
53 Back then
54 Nieuwpoort's river
56 On the ___ vive
57 Form 1040 org.

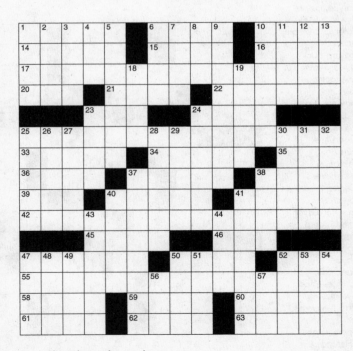

by John Underwood

ACROSS

1 "Madness" month
6 Crime-fighter Eliot Ness, notably
10 Hug givers
14 What a sun visor prevents
15 Saab or Subaru
16 Santa's "present" for a naughty child
17 Company that clears clogged drains
19 Game with Miss Scarlet and Professor Plum
20 "Faster!"
21 Spanish squiggle
22 Uses a stool
23 Phone part
25 Rocky hill
28 "____ on your life!"
29 Following
30 With 48-Across, popular computer product
32 Second Amendment rights org.
33 Adjective follower
36 Car for a star
37 Break, briefly . . . or a hint to this puzzle's theme
39 Use a keyboard
40 Held on to
41 Suffix with expert
42 Fancy tie
43 French political divisions
45 Barn bird
47 U.S.N.A. grad
48 See 30-Across
50 The Godfather's voice, e.g.
52 Put in ____ way
53 Scenic view
57 Greek Cupid
58 Friendly tournament format
60 Baseball's Matty or Felipe
61 Ladder step
62 1940s Bikini blast, in brief
63 Subject to mildew, perhaps
64 Web destination
65 Nick of "Lorenzo's Oil"

DOWN

1 Baseball team V.I.P.'s: Abbr.
2 Gobs
3 Assign an NC-17, e.g.
4 Corn and wheat
5 Nancy Drew or Joan of Arc
6 One who knows "the way"
7 Unlikely dog for a canine registry
8 Lunched, say
9 Neither's partner
10 Mishaps
11 Silver Cloud of autodom
12 Bea Arthur sitcom
13 Winter precipitation
18 Not fooled by
21 Explosive inits.
23 Steellike
24 Way off
25 Lecture
26 "Garfield" canine
27 Classic kids' show
31 Exhortation at a pub
32 SSW's opposite
34 Atop
35 New Jersey hoopsters
37 "Lovely ____, meter maid" (Beatles lyric)
38 Entry-level position: Abbr.
42 Ross Perot, in 1992 and 1996
44 Tummy muscles
45 Like pumpkins and traffic cones
46 Harry Potter prop
48 In front
49 Nurse Espinosa on "Scrubs"
51 Prefix with -plasm
53 Football kick
54 Cain's brother
55 Aerosol spray
56 Poker stake
58 Monopoly quartet: Abbr.
59 Pro vote in a French referendum

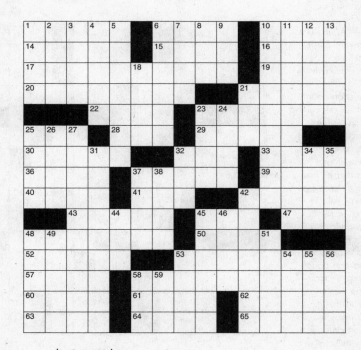

by Steve Kahn

ACROSS

1 Footlong sandwiches
5 Lost traction
9 Post office purchase
14 Fairy tale meanie
15 Hatcher of "Lois & Clark"
16 Himalayan kingdom
17 Short on dough
19 Play a role none too subtly
20 Kind of paper for gift-wrapping
21 Short on dough
23 ___ to stern
25 Dedicatory verse
26 Sports org. for scholars
29 Finger food at a Spanish restaurant
32 Over-the-top review
36 The "A" in A/V
38 Howard Stern's medium
40 Tiny criticism to "pick"
41 Short on dough
44 Part of an iceberg that's visible
45 Sarge's superior
46 Aquafina competitor
47 Aardvark's fare
49 Attack en masse, as a castle
51 Architect Saarinen
52 ___ Beta Kappa
54 Individually
56 Short on dough
61 Bits of wisdom?
65 One washing down a driveway, e.g.
66 Short on dough
68 Eye-teasing paintings
69 Saskatchewan Indian
70 Teeny bit
71 See 22-Down
72 "Thundering" group
73 Agts. looking for tax cheats

DOWN

1 Downy
2 Wrinkly fruit
3 Garments that usually clasp in the back
4 Takes off on a cruise
5 Avenue
6 Fierce type, astrologically
7 Annoys
8 Jenny Craig regimen
9 Three-time P.G.A. champ
10 Word repeated after someone starts to show anger
11 Individually
12 Chess ending
13 Begged
18 ". . . and nothing ___"
22 With 71-Across, "White Men Can't Jump" co-star
24 Ballet's Fonteyn
26 Can./U.S./Mex. treaty
27 Give hints to
28 Good (at)
30 Barbecue area
31 Stick (to)
33 "___ Get Your Gun"
34 Church official
35 Prefix with -centric
37 Something good to strike
39 Unclose, poetically
42 Polite refusal
43 "Enough already!"
48 Globe
50 In an atlas, e.g.
53 #1 to Avis's #2
55 So-so grade
56 Restaurant acronym
57 "Uh-uh"
58 Nicholas I or II
59 Do art on glass, say
60 Partner of truth
62 "A ___ of One's Own"
63 Instrument that's plucked
64 Baseball's ___ the Man
67 Individually

by Harriet Clifton

43

ACROSS

1 #1 number two who became the #2 number one
6 Actors who mug
10 Talking equine of '60s TV
14 Roll over, as a subscription
15 Neighbor of Yemen
16 Toy on a string
17 Food from heaven
18 Lot in life
19 ___-again (like some Christians)
20 She offered Excalibur to the future King Arthur
23 Garment accompanying a girdle
24 Last letter, in London
25 Gordon of "Oklahoma!"
29 Went out, as a fire
31 Club discussed in clubhouses: Abbr.
34 Guiding philosophy
35 Couch
36 Standard
37 Popular canned tuna
40 Word of invitation
41 Broadway award
42 Alleviates
43 Nile stinger
44 Hockey legend Gordie
45 Handles the food for the party
46 Big bird of the outback
47 Quilt locale
48 Columbia, in an old patriotic song
55 Witty Ephron
56 Lamb : ewe :: ___ : mare
57 Ram, astrologically

59 Voting no
60 Warren of the Supreme Court
61 Do, as a puzzle
62 Something to slip on?
63 Whirling current
64 County ENE of London

DOWN

1 Elbow's place
2 "Are we agreed?"
3 Late celebrity ___ Nicole Smith
4 Repair
5 Sag on a nag
6 Labor leader Jimmy who mysteriously disappeared
7 Amo, amas, ___ . . .
8 Trig or geometry

9 Take lightly
10 "Oops! I made a mistake"
11 Castle, in chess
12 "Jane ___"
13 "___ we now our gay apparel"
21 Valuable rock
22 ___ Zeppelin
25 Holy city of Islam
26 One of the Three Musketeers
27 Cheeta, in "Tarzan" films
28 Serving with chop suey
29 "Lorna ___"
30 Questionable
31 Rapper's entourage
32 Garson of "Mrs. Miniver"
33 Accumulate

35 The white in a whiteout
36 Tidy
38 Crayfish dish
39 One who could use a shrink
44 Medical care grp.
45 Corporate V.I.P.
46 EarthLink transmission
47 Stomach
48 Disappeared
49 Old Harper's Bazaar artist
50 Wart causer, in legend
51 Rocklike
52 Greek love god
53 Needs medicine
54 Campbell of "Scream"
55 40 winks
58 Topic for Dr. Ruth

by Randall J. Hartman

44

ACROSS

1 "Get out of here!"
5 Scott who draws "Dilbert"
10 Heart problem
14 Tortoise's race opponent
15 Argue against
16 Attempt at a basket
17 Fe, chemically
18 Actress Verdugo
19 Loving strokes
20 Course option
23 Hold the wheel
24 "___ So Fine," #1 Chiffons hit
25 Double curve
28 Old photo shade
32 Space cut by a scythe
34 ___ Khan
37 Response option
40 Ballet skirt
42 Dweller along the Volga
43 Signal hello or goodbye
44 Electric light option
47 Hedge plant
48 Person under 21
49 Group singing "Hallelujah!"
51 Sault ___ Marie
52 Stout drink
55 Parts to play
59 Quiz option
64 Advertising award
66 "Praise be to ___"
67 Lhasa ___
68 Easter servings
69 String bean's opposite
70 Person under 20
71 Optometrists' concerns
72 Department of ___
73 Ocean eagle

DOWN

1 Freighters, e.g.
2 Diamond weight
3 Came up
4 Tightens, with "up"
5 Space
6 Place to get an egg salad sandwich
7 Eve's second son
8 Chew (on)
9 Old hat
10 Nile nippers
11 Shoo off
12 Mouth-burning
13 Travelers from another galaxy, for short
21 Glenn of the Eagles
22 Professional grp.
26 Comedian Martin
27 "The Taming of the ___"
29 Consumers of Purina and Iams food
30 Vidi in "Veni, vidi, vici"
31 Playful trick
33 Opposite ENE
34 They're smashed in a smasher
35 "Go fast!," to a driver
36 Back then
38 Courtroom affirmation
39 Western U.S. gas giant
41 Carrier of 13-Down
45 Berlin Mrs.
46 Take on, as employees
50 Spin
53 Pages (through)
54 Key of Mozart's Symphony No. 39
56 Outcast
57 Ruhr Valley city
58 Gem
60 One of TV's "Friends"
61 ___ Vista (search engine)
62 Final
63 Mule or clog
64 Revolutionary Guevara
65 Make, as a wager

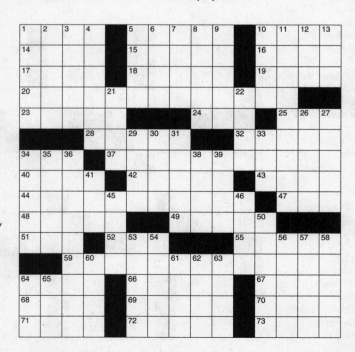

by Kurt Mengel and Jan-Michele Gianette

ACROSS

1 Gem units
7 Revolutionary Guevara
10 Sea creature that moves sideways
14 Common recipe amount
15 Actor Holbrook
16 Turner of Hollywood
17 Masonry work that may be smoothed with a trowel
19 Grace finisher
20 Deadly snake
21 Shoving away, football-style
23 Director Bob who won a Tony, Oscar and Emmy all in the same year
24 Evicts
25 Quester for the Golden Fleece
28 Hen's place
30 "It's a sin to tell ___"
31 Goes 80, say
34 Fellow
37 More rain and less light, e.g., to a pilot
40 Sault ___ Marie
41 Ill-___ gains
42 Hitchhiker's need
43 Tabbies
44 Person whose name appears on a museum plaque, e.g.
45 Zorro's weapon
48 Colorado resort
51 Some memorization in arithmetic class
54 Airport overseer: Abbr.
57 Director Kazan
58 Earlier . . . or a hint to the words circled in 17-, 21-, 37- and 51-Across

60 Book after John
61 Coach Parseghian
62 White fur
63 Two tablets every six hours, e.g.
64 Thieve
65 Target and J. C. Penney

DOWN

1 ___ Nostra
2 Six-legged intruders
3 Sign on, as for another tour of duty
4 N.C. State's group
5 University of Arizona's home
6 Leopard markings
7 Rub raw
8 .5
9 Singer Fitzgerald
10 Zip one's lip
11 Harold who directed "Groundhog Day"
12 Concerning
13 Hair over the forehead
18 State known for its cheese: Abbr.
22 Hen's place
23 Enemies
25 1975 thriller that took a big bite at the box office
26 Very much
27 Father
28 Give
29 Chief Norse god
31 Many a person whose name starts Mac
32 Flower holders
33 Suffix with differ
34 Enter

35 Ruin
36 Belgian river to the North Sea
38 "Zounds!"
39 Laundry implement that might make a 43-Down
43 See 39-Down
44 Gobi or Mojave
45 Lieu
46 Radio word after "Roger"
47 Skips
48 Popular BBC import, for short
49 ___-mo replay
50 Israel's Shimon
52 Skier's transport
53 Prefix with -nautic
54 Light-skinned
55 Actress Heche
56 Citrus coolers
59 M.D.'s group

by Peter A. Collins

ACROSS

1 Padlocked fasteners
6 Diet drink phrase
11 Beaver's work
14 God to a Muslim
15 Ralph's wife on "The Honeymooners"
16 Brazilian hot spot
17 Levy on consumer goods
19 I love: Lat.
20 Rock concert blasters
21 Web address ender
22 Shovel user
24 Chopped liver spread
26 Makes safe
27 "Evita" star Patti
30 ___ Quimby (Beverly Cleary heroine)
31 Dizzying designs
32 Most common throw with two dice
33 "Moo" maker
36 Cut and paste, say
37 Starts of 17- and 55-Across and 11- and 29-Down, impolitely
38 Knotty wood
39 Rockers ___ Jovi
40 Red-tag events
41 Explorer ___ de León
42 Popular candy bar
44 Stuck out
45 Source of a licoricelike flavoring
47 Piece of rodeo gear
48 Fountain treat
49 Have the flu, maybe
50 Was a fink
54 Humorist Shriner
55 Exterminator's work
58 Street crosser: Abbr.
59 Songstress Gorme
60 Striker's demand
61 "So's ___ old man!"
62 Hatchlings' homes
63 Cosmetician Elizabeth

DOWN

1 Mandlikova of tennis
2 Homecoming attendee, for short
3 Woman's undergarment
4 Globetrotter's document
5 Oldies group ___ Na Na
6 Mother-of-pearl
7 Cassini of fashion
8 Op. ___ (footnote abbr.)
9 College professors, e.g.
10 Dictionary
11 Activity on a strip
12 Actress Anouk
13 Othello's people
18 Post-it message
23 Pistol, e.g.
25 Aardvark's morsel
26 Doesn't spend everything
27 Leopold's co-defendant in 1920s crime
28 High hair style
29 Morphine, e.g.
30 Convened anew
32 "Rabbit food"
34 Years back
35 Lawn intruder
37 Unaided sight
38 Guiding light
40 Increase in verticality
41 Young seal
43 Believer's suffix
44 Tie with a clasp
45 Home products seller
46 Artless
47 Reduces to bits
49 Going ___ (bickering)
51 Dry as dust
52 Scent detector
53 Secluded valley
56 '60s protest grp.
57 Pro-Second Amendment grp.

by Fred Piscop

ACROSS

1 Prison division
5 Prevalent
9 Ludicrous comedy
14 Tennis's Nastase
15 Make in income
16 Full of activity
17 Jam-packed with laughs and entertainment
19 Activist Chavez
20 "Sounds good to me!"
21 Yadda yadda yadda
23 Bean counter, for short
24 Remove, as a hat
25 Result of overexercise
28 ___ Paulo, Brazil
30 Checking out, as before a robbery
35 Dude
36 ___ fatale
38 Unusual object
39 Gridiron game with imaginary teams
42 Chilean range
43 Congestion location
44 Proof finale
45 Actor Warren
47 Prime meridian std.
48 Leaning Tower city
49 Porgy and bass
51 By way of
53 "Hurry up!"
57 Available, as a doctor
61 Nintendo's ___ Bros.
62 One way to jump in a pool
64 Turn topsy-turvy
65 Not made up
66 In the vicinity
67 Orals, e.g.

68 Lith. and Ukr., formerly
69 Bagful for Dobbin

DOWN

1 Modern kind of network
2 College grad
3 Saturn feature
4 Scrawl graffiti on, e.g.
5 Puts out, as a record
6 Suffix with president
7 Some guerrillas
8 Put an ___ (halt)
9 Be realistic
10 Help in a getaway, e.g.
11 Deception
12 Powerful person

13 Book after II Chronicles
18 Little scamp
22 Ozone depleter, for short
25 '90s Brit sitcom
26 See 33-Down
27 Civic maker
29 The Carters' daughter and others
31 Footlong, e.g.
32 Baghdad resident
33 With 26-Down, "Frasier" character
34 Mideast's Meir
36 Fare at KFC, McDonald's, Burger King, etc.
37 Geologic periods
40 Asian holiday

41 Defeats at the ballot box
46 Yang's counterpart
48 Al of "Insomnia," 2002
50 Sorts (through)
52 Like Beethoven's "Pastoral" Symphony
53 Dirty reading
54 Surveillance evidence
55 "You are" in Spain
56 Pub serving
58 Department
59 Future atty.'s exam
60 P.O. items
63 Where Switz. is

by Curtis Yee

48

ACROSS

1 E-mail from a Nigerian with $10 million to give you, e.g.
5 Average
9 Dwarf planet whose name is a Disney character
14 Loser to the tortoise
15 ___ vera
16 Poe bird
17 Clapton who sang "Layla"
18 ___ Hari (spy)
19 Musical work featuring 3-Down
20 State flower of Maryland
23 Light into
24 Kind of number: Abbr.
25 Flower with large velvety clusters
32 Sweetie
35 Words of comparison
36 Southwest plant
37 Much
39 Request from a doctor with a tongue depressor
42 Pagoda instrument
43 Late princess
45 Said aloud
47 Born: Fr.
48 Flower in the violet family often seen on roadsides
52 Prefix with thermal
53 Grand and baby grand
57 Frilly white flower also called wild carrot
62 It makes scents
63 "Open late" sign, maybe
64 Old balladeer's instrument
65 Wash off
66 "Otello" baritone
67 City east of Utah Lake
68 Quickness
69 Historic school on the Thames
70 Deep grooves

DOWN

1 Biblical land with a queen
2 Olympic track gold medalist Lewis et al.
3 Songs in a 19-Across
4 Places people are drawn to
5 Anonymous
6 Oil of ___
7 Repetitive process
8 Pasture
9 How a peacock struts?
10 Trips around the track
11 Eye part
12 Bird with a forked tail
13 Put ___ show
21 Fuzzy green fruit
22 ___ Lanka
26 Greek "H"
27 "Happy birthday ___"
28 Haul
29 Much-respected person
30 Clearasil target
31 Sorcerer
32 Muslim pilgrimage
33 Mishmash
34 He released a dove in Genesis
38 Old cable inits.
40 Sling's contents
41 Discover accidentally
44 Irate
46 San ___ Obispo, Calif.
49 Tokyo money
50 "Happy Days" character
51 Wanness
54 Pacific nation once known as Pleasant Island
55 Group of eight
56 Appears
57 Common cosmetics applicator
58 Eclectic magazine Reader
59 Lighten, as a burden
60 In apple-pie order
61 Aborted
62 "___ Poetica"

by Raymond Hamel

ACROSS

1 Untidiness
5 Gillette razor
9 Felt good about
14 Border on
15 Karate blow
16 ___ Pendragon, King Arthur's father
17 Crime bigwig
18 Genuine
19 Beauty queen's headgear
20 "The Man Who . . ." (1956)
23 Basinger of "Batman"
24 Cincinnati team
25 Homo sapiens, for man
27 Jogged
29 Ladder rung
32 Jackie's second spouse
33 Sightings the U.S.A.F. may investigate
35 Notion
37 Debate
41 "The Man Who . . ." (1973)
44 Muse of love poetry
45 Cruel
46 Time ___ half
47 Bird that hoots
49 Actress Meg
51 Deity
52 England/France connection
56 Give up, as territory
58 ___ Tin Tin
59 "The Man Who . . ." (1976)
64 Musical with the song "Don't Cry for Me, Argentina"
66 Long, long time
67 Seldom seen
68 Bit in a bed of roses
69 Repair
70 Hip bones
71 '50s Ford flop
72 Neighborhood
73 Boy ___ door

DOWN

1 Ted with TV's old "Original Amateur Hour"
2 Abba of Israel
3 Exploding star
4 Vermont ski resort
5 Verse with a hidden message
6 Lt. Kojak on "Kojak"
7 Wander
8 Great grade
9 Protestant who believes in the Book of Concord
10 "Lord, is ___?"
11 Park ranger's uniform color
12 Spine-tingling
13 Apothecaries' units
21 N.F.L. scores
22 Asst. on taxes
26 About
27 Reign
28 Get an ___ effort
30 Dutch cheese
31 Paul and Mary's partner in folk music
34 ___ Hall University
36 "An apple ___ keeps . . ."
38 Canada Dry product
39 Destroy
40 Old oath
42 Waterloo
43 Amazon menace
48 Harper who wrote "To Kill a Mockingbird"
50 Jacqueline Kennedy ___ Bouvier
52 Breakfast item with syrup
53 Made a home, as bees
54 The U's in B.T.U.'s
55 Andean animal
57 Bobby who sang "Beyond the Sea"
60 Sideways glance
61 Musical signal
62 Cereal with a rabbit mascot
63 Oven setting
65 Menlo Park inits.

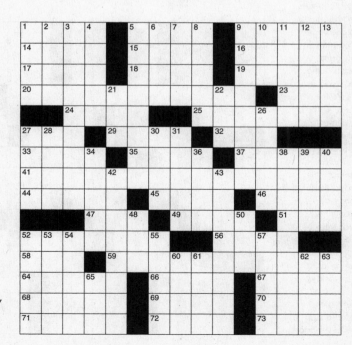

by Randy Sowell

ACROSS

1 "___ Las Vegas" (1964 Elvis movie)
5 Armageddon
9 Snapshot
14 Gulf of ___, off the coast of Yemen
15 River of Spain
16 Pavarotti, notably
17 First digit in a California ZIP code
18 Hammer's end
19 ___-Seltzer
20 Those seeking attention?
23 Had a bite
24 Obstinate one
25 Convoy's front
29 Rapper Dr. ___
30 Waterfall effect
31 Cheer for a torero
32 Hearth contents
35 Dobbin's dinner
36 Skin cream ingredient
37 Mark on a Russian author's to-do list?
40 Gen. Patton, to George C. Scott
41 Pod contents
42 Subtle reminders
43 First lady?
44 Casino card game
45 Five-spot
46 Graduates-to-be
48 Chaney of horror films
49 U-turn from NNW
52 A Bangkok drink I had?
55 Clean in a tub
58 Go beyond a once-over
59 Make yawn
60 TV studio sign
61 Algerian seaport
62 Jai ___
63 Twists out of shape

64 What it may take to answer the question "Does this make me look fat?"
65 City near Carson City

DOWN

1 Title uncle in a classic Russian play
2 Doofus
3 Show's place
4 Once more
5 Topple, as a ruler
6 Follows directions
7 Splittable cookie
8 Single-slab stone monuments
9 J.F.K. commanded one in W.W. II
10 He ordered the execution of John the Baptist
11 Lennon's Yoko
12 Mr. Turkey
13 El Dorado's treasure
21 Like an arctic winter
22 Hermann who wrote "Siddhartha"
26 :
27 In the air
28 Snorkeling destinations
29 Hockey player's deceptive move
30 Former Portuguese territory in 39-Down
32 1960s TV's "Green ___"
33 Subway rider's move
34 Hunt of "As Good as It Gets"
35 Go too far
36 Related (to)
38 Dizzying museum display
39 Home to 1.3 billion people
44 Gathering spots at intermission
45 Instigate
47 "Gotcha, bro"
48 Shade of purple
49 Ripped off
50 Food wrap
51 Old MacDonald refrain
53 Taj Mahal site
54 Letter-shaped girder
55 Arrow's shooter
56 Santa ___, Calif.
57 Road goo

by Randall J. Hartman

ACROSS

1 President pro ___
4 Back biter?
9 ___ Polo, visitor to Cathay
14 Manipulate
15 Bad treatment
16 Flip one's lid?
17 Record label with a dog in its logo
18 Prove false
19 Movers and shakers
20 Outlaw William + actor Alan = Scottish boy?
23 Neither's go-with
24 Bay window
25 ___ the pants off
27 ___-mo replay
29 Pittsburgh team
33 Loud speaker
35 New Mexico art community
37 Hopping mad
38 Archaeologist Louis + actress Farrah = job for a plumber?
43 Huge mistake
44 Plummet
45 Lives
47 Declared
53 Minister, slangily
54 Sushi fish
56 Skedaddle
57 Guy's date
59 Wit Oscar + writer Joyce Carol = things to sow?
63 "Dig?"
65 Supermodel Campbell
66 Suffix with differ
67 Perfume
68 ___ Island, immigrants' arrival point
69 Karel Capek drama
70 The Evita of "Evita"
71 Nick of "Lorenzo's Oil"
72 Hush-hush job

DOWN

1 Supercharged engines
2 Accompany to a party
3 No Mr. Nice Guy
4 Onetime phone company nickname
5 Toe the line
6 Break in the action
7 Continent explored by 9-Across
8 Oboe and bassoon
9 Wet dirt
10 Ever and ___
11 Brightness regulator
12 Singer Vikki + senator Trent = auto site?
13 Extra play periods, for short
21 Maiden name preceder
22 Twosome
26 Clapton who sang "Layla"
28 Lode load
30 Summer on the Riviera
31 They're soaked up at the beach
32 Capital of Bulgaria
34 "___ you nuts?"
36 Without: Fr.
38 Actor Rob + actor Richard = something to put a truck in?
39 One way to get up in the world?
40 Everything
41 MacLachlan of "Twin Peaks"
42 Divs. of a year
43 New Deal pres.
46 Stitch (up)
48 Plaza Hotel girl of fiction
49 Stephen of "Michael Collins"
50 Spuds
51 Align the edges of
52 "___ Rides Again" (1939 western)
55 Tablecloths
58 Chauffeur-driven vehicle
60 Film composer Schifrin
61 Barbie, e.g.
62 Give off
63 Opening
64 Beachgoer's shade

by Randall J. Hartman

52

ACROSS

1 Rollick or frolic
5 Singer Seeger
9 It's a no-no
14 Cleveland's lake
15 "Roots" writer Haley
16 Summer TV fare
17 Eat
18 Crossworder's crutch: Abbr.
19 Hopping mad
20 Did accounting hanky-panky, to a housekeeper?
23 Chicken ___ king
24 Loaf with seeds
25 Free (of)
26 Letters after els
28 Prefix with -gon
30 Variety, in life, so it's said
32 Visage overlooking Tiananmen Square
33 Made in the ___
35 ___ v. Wade
36 Belgrade resident
37 Did crime scene work, to a housekeeper?
42 Popular pizza/grill chain, informally
43 Newsman Rather
44 Speaks, informally
45 Thirsty
46 Hägar the Horrible's wife
48 Greek moralist
52 ... --- ...
53 &
54 W–Z, e.g., in an encyc.
56 "Able was I ___ ..."
57 Handled Mob finances, to a housekeeper?
61 Threw
62 Cape Town currency
63 Cartoon opossum
64 Right-hand page
65 Chills and fever
66 Jog
67 Classic theater
68 Immodest look
69 Right-minded

DOWN

1 Baggage porter
2 Camden Yards player
3 Dweller on ancient Crete
4 What not to do before December 25?
5 Rice field
6 Upper crusts
7 Kind of support
8 Outside
9 Certain vacuum tube
10 Prefix with nautical
11 Some railroaders
12 Defeat with cunning
13 Air Force ___
21 Rub out
22 Muscle that's often shown off
27 Blubbers
29 Sounds of reproof
31 Part of a fork
34 Part of a sum
36 Petite or jumbo
37 Bombs without bangs
38 Opened, as a carpet
39 Chow mein flavorer
40 Nonsense: Var.
41 Domain
46 "Not so fast!"
47 Madison in New York or New York in Washington
49 Title in Tijuana
50 Beaver State
51 Mescaline source
55 Weirder
58 Golden rule preposition
59 Fury
60 Chooses (to)
61 Bushy do, for short

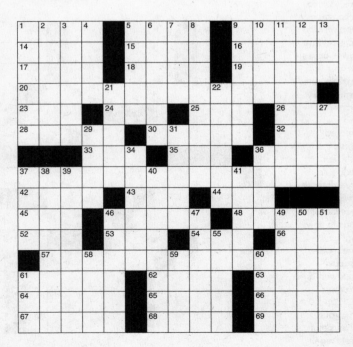

by Larry Paul

ACROSS

1 Lacking face value, as stock
6 For fear that
10 "The doctor ___"
14 Speechify
15 Blues singer James
16 ___ extra cost
17 Discotheque performer
19 The "N" of N.B.A.: Abbr.
20 ___ Gay (W.W. II plane)
21 Get sleepy-eyed
23 "Norma ___" (Sally Field film)
24 Extinct bird
26 Walking the dog and others
29 Up in the air
31 Schlep
32 Lenten symbol
33 Never-before-seen
34 Hockey star Lindros
36 Nine-digit ID
37 1920s musical with the sequel "Yes, Yes, Yvette"
41 Sombrero, e.g.
42 "Beloved" author Morrison
43 Mover's vehicle
46 One more time
49 Prosecutors, for short
50 Cream cheese flavoring
52 Haute couture icon with her own perfume
55 Dairy case item
56 Hanoi holiday
57 Chatter
58 PC storage medium
60 Brezhnev's land, in brief
62 It might have two stars
66 Slightly
67 "Bring ___!"
68 Bright bunch
69 Red ink entry
70 London gallery
71 "A burger, fries and a large Coke," e.g.

DOWN

1 Yuletide beverage
2 Conquistador's treasure
3 Scroll key on a computer
4 Many, many
5 Make over
6 "Chocolat" actress
7 And so on: Abbr.
8 Shorthand specialist, for short
9 Fortuneteller's card
10 Fleming who created 007
11 Shirt stiffener
12 Amount eaten
13 At a minimum
18 Prince ___ Khan
22 Severe
24 Former CBS anchor Rather
25 Corrida call
27 Mexican peninsula
28 Stevie Wonder's "___ She Lovely"
30 Period of a renter's lease
35 Balderdash
36 One of 100 on Capitol Hill: Abbr.
38 Birthplace of seven U.S. presidents
39 Front section of a rocket
40 Lex Luthor, for one
44 St. crossing
45 Prefix with classical
46 Genuine
47 Attends
48 Pretends to be
49 End of two state names
51 Loser to Roosevelt in 1932
53 ___ coming (warrants punishment)
54 King or emir: Abbr.
59 San ___ (Riviera resort)
61 Hwys.
63 Tippler
64 Language suffix
65 1970 #1 hit with the lyric "huh, yeah, What is it good for?"

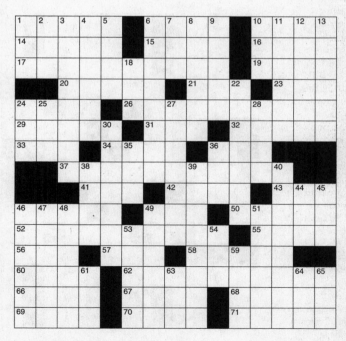

by Richard Chisholm

54

ACROSS

1 House in Spain
5 Keach of the small screen
10 Peter the Great, for one
14 European auto
15 Machine shop tool
16 River to the Seine
17 Little ___, Dickens girl
18 Place for sketches
20 Introduction in a Dr. Seuss book
22 Go on all fours
23 Coffee dispenser
24 Computer data holders
28 Order that may be scrambled or sunny-side up
30 Passed, as laws
32 Onetime Illinois governor Stevenson
34 "See ya!"
35 Golfer Ernie
36 Introduction in "Moby-Dick"
40 U.S./Gr. Brit. separator
41 6 on a phone pad
42 Answer
43 Like Marcel Duchamp's "Mona Lisa"
46 Jolt provider in a car
47 Typical Court TV programming
48 Berlin's land: Abbr.
50 Showbiz twin Mary-Kate or Ashley
54 Introduction in an NBC sitcom
57 Cleans up financially
60 100%
61 Line of rotation
62 Dweebs
63 Like ___ not
64 ___ messaging (modern communication)
65 Judge the value of, as ore
66 Congers

DOWN

1 Shaped like a dunce cap
2 ". . . partridge in ___ tree"
3 1965 Alabama march site
4 "Things are fine . . ."
5 Door-closing sound
6 Set of foot bones
7 Perfume from petals
8 Passageways for Santa
9 "Can" opener?
10 "Like wow, man"
11 Five-digit number on an envelope
12 Happy ___ lark
13 Ketchup-colored
19 "Look, I did it!"
21 Like pond scum
25 Stainless ___
26 Clarkson who won the first "American Idol"
27 Radical '60s grp.
29 "Hand it over, buster!"
31 First P.M. of modern India
32 Thespian
33 ___ Lama
34 Life story
37 Chess finales
38 Office messages
39 With mom, symbol of Americanism
40 15-percenter: Abbr.
44 Least wild
45 Tarzan player Ron and others
46 Starr of the comics
49 Mideast leaders
51 Cook, as onions
52 Swashbuckler Flynn
53 Mets and Cubs, for short
55 "Peter Pan" dog
56 ___-bitsy
57 Small rug
58 Logger's tool
59 General Mills cereal

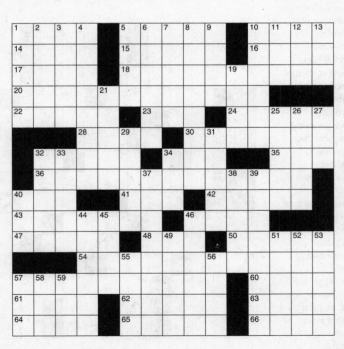

by Elizabeth C. Gorski

ACROSS

1 Jewel
4 Accumulate
9 One making a point at church?
14 Mine find
15 Money in India
16 Hearing-related
17 Top-ranked player in a tournament
19 Little old man in a fairy tale
20 Supernatural
21 Confucian path
23 Network that covers the N.Y.S.E.
24 Reward from a boss
25 Holdup victim's plea
27 Kids' guessing game
29 Cereal that's "for kids"
30 Smoker's mouthpiece
34 Shoot using a scope, say
37 Ripken who played 2,632 straight games
38 Dutch island in the Caribbean
41 Playa ___ Rey, Calif.
42 Trap
45 Decorative foil
48 Cheap laughs
50 Patricia ___, Best Actress for "Hud"
51 Beer drinker's bar request
55 "Of course," slangily
59 See 60-Across
60 With 59-Across, battle planning site
61 Pay no heed
62 Kofi of the U.N.
64 Pilgrims' carrier

66 Long, drawn-out attack
67 Indifferent
68 Dig into, as dinner
69 Check recipient
70 Furrier John Jacob ___
71 Area between N. and S. Korea

DOWN

1 Try to attain
2 "Fear of Fifty" writer Jong
3 Parisian thanks
4 Lacking guile
5 Be compelled to
6 Cousin of a human
7 Look after
8 Alternative to a convertible
9 Slump
10 Hit the time clock
11 Rust
12 Classic Stallone role
13 Send to the Capitol
18 "Wake Up Little ___"
22 Hall-of-Famer Mel
25 Easter egg decorator
26 Sophs., two years later
28 Mom-and-pop grp.
30 Dell products
31 Singer Janis
32 Monopoly game equipment
33 Face on a "wanted" poster
35 Vegetable on a vine
36 North Pole helper

39 School funder, often
40 Drink with a head on it
43 Search (through)
44 Squeeze (out)
46 Tassel on a cap, e.g.
47 Grassy plain of South America
49 Logging tool
51 Understanding
52 Ancient region with an architectural style named after it
53 "La ___" ('59 hit)
54 European/Asian range
56 Dragged behind
57 Cat's saucerful
58 Avis rival
61 "In that case . . ."
63 Born: Fr.
65 China's Sun ___-sen

by Lynn Lempel

56

ACROSS

1 High-I.Q. group
6 Pennsylvania university, for short
10 Change, as the décor
14 Island with a reef
15 Sound in a cave
16 Allege
17 Got fit, with "up"
18 23-Across's representative in the 38-Across
20 Battery terminal
21 The New World: Abbr.
22 Howe'er
23 One of two parties to 38-Across
27 He can go to blazes
30 Cries convulsively
31 W.C. in London
32 "Cómo ___?"
34 Dog in "The Thin Man"
38 Declaration of August 14, 1941, regarding peace aims after W.W. II
43 Island east of Java
44 "Little piggies"
45 "Exodus" hero
46 Scholastic sports grp.
50 Common entree at a potluck dinner
52 One of two parties to 38-Across
56 Silent assent
57 Arnaz of 1950s TV
58 Biblical land with a queen
62 52-Across's representative in the 38-Across
65 Spreader of seeds

66 ___ of Wight
67 Plenty mad
68 Build
69 Mole, to a gardener
70 Bygone Fords
71 Library stations

DOWN

1 ___ Hari (W.W. I spy)
2 School for Prince William
3 Taboo
4 Heavy hitter
5 Municipal lawmakers
6 Chest muscle, for short
7 Popular Apple communication software
8 Hitchhikers' digits
9 Caped fighter
10 Word of cheer
11 The second Mrs. Perón
12 Indian city of 12+ million
13 Acrylic fiber
19 Place for a mobile
24 90° from north
25 One who hasn't turned pro?
26 Old Russian monarch
27 Spare tire
28 Not one ___
29 Somersault
33 Do something
35 Antlered animal
36 Seabird with a forked tail
37 Opera solo
39 Fats Waller's "___ Misbehavin'"

40 Pepsi, e.g.
41 Summer woe
42 Evaluated
47 Give up
48 Have ___ of a time
49 Declare
51 On the beach
52 Tear open, as seams
53 Loop with a slipknot
54 Hero types
55 Like most bathroom floors
59 Wool coat wearers
60 Call's partner
61 Word with liberal or martial
63 Call between ready and go
64 Six-pointers, for short

by Gene Newman

ACROSS

1 Capital of Tibet
6 [Oh, my heavens!]
10 "Get lost, kitty!"
14 String ties
15 Sharif of film
16 Tiny bit
17 Sound after a tear is shed
18 Shoestring
19 Unappetizing food
20 Parental demand #1
23 Major leaguer
24 British rocker Brian
25 Actor Beatty
26 Sheet of ice
29 Putin's rejection
32 Sets (down)
34 Parachute part
35 Grooved on
36 Lobbying grp.
37 Parental demand #2
43 General at Appomattox
44 ___ favor (please, in Spanish)
45 Gumbo vegetable
46 "Gee willikers!"
48 Surmounting
49 "Hey . . . you!"
50 Cousin of "ruff!"
51 Column's counterpart
53 "Well, ___-di-dah!"
55 Parental demand #3
61 Supply-and-demand subj.
62 Long car, for short
63 Construction piece
65 Salon job
66 Mishmash
67 Fine thread
68 Sequoia, for one
69 New Jersey hoopsters
70 Kid's response to 20-, 37- and 55-Across

DOWN

1 Abbr. on a dumbbell
2 ___ Kong
3 "That's ___!" (debate retort)
4 Plays down, as an issue
5 In reference to
6 Sport with woods and Woods
7 Part of a Latin 101 conjugation
8 Scented pouch
9 Fuss over oneself
10 [Isn't he dreamy?!]
11 Massachusetts, e.g., before 1776
12 Makes amends
13 Not live
21 Dipping dish
22 Like Peary's explorations
26 Govt. media watchdog
27 Chat room joke response
28 Miner's load
30 Nope's counterpart
31 Pharaoh's land
33 Woe on an observation deck
36 Lilac or violet
38 India's first P.M.
39 Tic-tac-toe win
40 Green-lights
41 Surgery sites, for short
42 "Welcome" site
46 Worker with an apron
47 From way back when
48 For some time
50 Skillful
52 Synthetic fiber
54 "Where there's ___ . . ."
56 "This one's ___!"
57 Fail to mention
58 Dairy farm sounds
59 Take a break
60 Cabbagelike vegetable
64 Mal de ___

by Elayne Cantor

58

ACROSS

1 Bullets and such
5 High-tech appt. books
9 Duo times four
14 Gather, as grain
15 The New Yorker cartoonist Peter
16 Plant life
17 "It's true!" (#1)
20 Shorthand pro, for short
21 Cousin of contra-
22 "The King and I" heroine
23 Emcee
25 "I get it, stop nagging me!"
27 Chinese temples
30 Leap day's mo.
31 Astern
34 Rights org.
35 Hooey
37 Prefix with continental
39 "It's true!" (#2)
43 Places to build on
44 Crew member's implement
45 Ends up with
46 Abbr. on a golf scorecard
47 ___ green
50 Palestine's locale
52 U.N. member through 1991
53 Leave port
54 Verdon of Broadway
57 Hemingway nickname
59 Greedy king of myth
63 "It's true!" (#3)
66 Fable's end
67 Where the Euphrates flows
68 Give off
69 Skiing locale
70 Cows chew them
71 Installs, as an outfield

DOWN

1 Sciences' partner
2 Beef or bacon
3 Cobble together
4 Realtor's event
5 Be worthwhile
6 Baker St. assistant
7 Poetic adverb
8 In a way
9 Not quite oneself
10 Part of a Dracula costume
11 Unable to decide
12 Nickname for Ireland
13 Informal farewell
18 Frame of mind
19 Flood protector
24 Calcutta attire
26 Newspaper notice
27 Unwitting victim
28 Sharply stinging
29 Overstuffs
31 Between ports
32 Outstanding accomplishments
33 Secret meeting
36 A wee hour
38 Cat's asset, it's said
40 Recipe amts.
41 Post-Easter sandwich content
42 Puccini piece
48 Fox Sports alternative
49 Official language of Libya
51 Thin coin
52 Open, as a toothpaste tube
54 Workout centers
55 Scarf material
56 Money in Madrid
58 Cuzco's country
60 Floor model
61 In the thick of
62 Collect-'em-all collections
64 Drink on draught
65 Mental measures, for short

by Stanley Newman

ACROSS

1 Part of a flower or wineglass
5 "Exodus" author Leon
9 "Aladdin" villain
14 Volcano output
15 Quarter of a bushel
16 Had dinner at home
17 Jai ___
18 Sycamore or cypress
19 Diploma receivers, for short
20 The best place to sleep
23 Drought relief
24 This-and-that dish
25 Most strange
28 They may be tapped for fraternities
32 Singer in ABBA
33 Give up a poker hand
34 "Vive le ___!"
35 The best place to sit
39 Vietnamese New Year
40 Abhor
41 Make up (for)
42 Long journeys
45 Name holders
46 "Little piggies"
47 About, on a memo
48 The best place to see
54 Narrow openings
55 Ending with peek or bug
56 Place to order a ham on rye
57 Secret stash
58 Take care of, as a store

59 Prez, e.g.
60 Like a stamp pad
61 Guitarist Townshend
62 Carve in stone

DOWN

1 Response to a rude remark
2 A fisherman might bring back a big one
3 Sen. Bayh of Indiana
4 They show you to your table
5 Ready for a challenge
6 Second airing
7 Summer coolers in tiny cups
8 ___-Ball (arcade game)

9 Alternative to a Mercedes or BMW
10 In jeopardy
11 Burlesque show accessory
12 Capitol Hill worker
13 E.R. workers
21 Attacks
22 Loses hair, as a dog
25 "We're ___ See the Wizard"
26 Hung on the clothesline
27 Prank that's not nice
28 Yachts, e.g.
29 Otherwise
30 On one's way
31 Trig functions
33 Whip

36 Where VapoRub may be rubbed
37 Training group
38 Conference-goer
43 Relieve
44 Felt
45 Like secret messages
47 "Not gonna do it"
48 Custard dessert
49 Highway exit
50 Theater award
51 Student's book
52 Monthly util. bill
53 Having megamillions
54 Chem. or biol.

by Mike Nothnagel

60

ACROSS

1 Blind trio in a children's rhyme
5 Cripples
10 Hindu prince
14 On the ocean
15 Eve of "Our Miss Brooks"
16 "Be it ___ so humble . . ."
17 Tenant's monthly check
18 Embroidery, e.g.
20 Crosses (out)
21 Wrote fraudulently, as a check
22 Armored vehicles
23 Chicago-based TV talk show
25 Actor Bert in a lion's suit
27 Lantern usable during storms
31 Snaky curves
32 Activist Brockovich
33 Mauna ___ (Hawaiian volcano)
36 Like arson evidence
37 Bread for breakfast
39 Bucket
40 Prefix with cycle
41 Closed
42 Refuse a request
43 Hanukkah food
47 Dramatist Simon who wrote "Plaza Suite"
48 Rewords
49 Tolerate
52 Fable writer
54 Olympic gold-medal runner Sebastian
57 Some makeup
59 Alluring
60 Actor Baldwin
61 Hackneyed
62 Leg's midpoint
63 Hazard
64 Without the help of written music
65 Hankerings

DOWN

1 Karl who philosophized about class struggle
2 "Aha!"
3 Government suppression of the press
4 Have dinner
5 Nutcase
6 Franklin known as the Queen of Soul
7 ___ fixe (obsession)
8 Busybodies
9 Weekend NBC hit, for short
10 Put on the stove again
11 The Bard's river
12 Bozo
13 Torah holders
19 Wharton's "___ Frome"
21 ___ Kringle
24 Hunter's target
26 Landed (on)
27 Summer oppressiveness
28 SALT I signer
29 "Cool!"
30 Do some acting
34 Sty sound
35 ___ vera
37 Spicy Asian cuisine
38 Criminal activity
39 Treaty
41 Precipitous
42 Small scissor cut
44 Next up
45 Pre-euro Spanish coin
46 Worshipful one
49 Way, way off
50 "___ Ha'i" ("South Pacific" song)
51 Frosty desserts
53 ___ Britt on "Desperate Housewives"
55 Yoked beasts
56 What the starts of 18-, 27-, 43- and 57-Across all have
58 Wagering loc.
59 Heavens

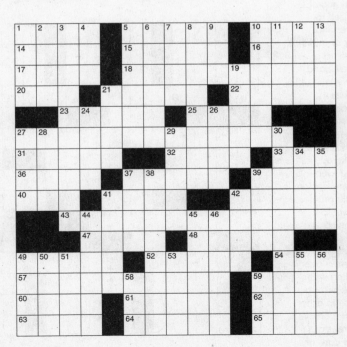

by Lynn Lempel

ACROSS

1 Comedian Foxworthy
5 Tiff
9 Manhandle
14 Early TV role for Ron Howard
15 Author Victor
16 Comment to the audience
17 1960s series about a boy and his bear
19 Outsides of lemons and limes
20 12th-grader
21 Swiss-based relief group
23 Johnny of "Pirates of the Caribbean"
25 Itsy-bitsy
26 Choose
29 Greeting with a hug and a kiss, say
35 Cawing birds
37 Go bankrupt
38 Ever and ___
39 Kind of lamp at a luau
40 Composer Franz
41 Give temporarily
42 Genesis garden
43 ___ Major
44 Popeye's burly foe
45 Feature of the Christian God
48 Cathedral seat
49 Dernier ___ (the latest thing)
50 Cold and damp, as a basement
52 Home of a hypothetical monster
57 "I haven't the foggiest"
61 Miss ___ of TV's "Dallas"
62 Compliment
64 Grabs (onto)

65 Object of devotion
66 Mailed
67 "Full House" actor Bob
68 Being nothing more than
69 "The Bridge on the River ___"

DOWN

1 Runs for exercise
2 Sporting sword
3 Huckleberry ___
4 Offensive-smelling
5 Mountain climber's guide
6 Place to play darts
7 Chemical used by document forgers
8 Dial ___
9 Package
10 "If memory serves . . ."
11 Overindulger of the grape
12 Throws in
13 ___ Trueheart of "Dick Tracy"
18 Big name in movie theaters
22 Lived (in)
24 Employer of flacks
26 Santa's reindeer, minus Rudolph
27 Egotist's sin
28 Subway coin
30 En ___ (as a group)
31 Harry Potter, for one
32 Outdo by a little
33 Three-card scam
34 Furnish with a fund
36 Porch music maker

40 Alison who won a Pulitzer for "Foreign Affairs"
44 Previously, up to this point
46 Polar explorer Shackleton
47 Wick holder
51 Newsstand
52 Chicken drumsticks
53 Earthenware pot
54 Job for a drain cleaner
55 Read over hurriedly
56 Pro or con
58 Provoked, as enemy fire
59 Poet ___ St. Vincent Millay
60 Wine-producing region of Italy
63 Neither hide ___ hair

by Dave Tuller

62

ACROSS

1 Word repeated before "black sheep, have you any wool?"
4 Semester
8 Seizes (from)
14 Building add-on
15 Downwind, on a ship
16 Kitt who played Catwoman on "Batman"
17 Avg., sizewise
18 Aromatherapy liquid
20 Cereal named for two ingredients it doesn't have
22 ___ of Cleves, English queen
23 Back of a boat
24 Emergency PC key
25 SSW's reverse
26 The "I" in T.G.I.F.
28 Jacuzzi
31 Jacuzzis
34 Maxima maker
38 "Put ___ Happy Face"
39 Really tired
42 Small bed
43 Followed the leader
44 Shady giants
45 Becomes a parent not by childbirth
47 Slangy assent
49 "Once upon a midnight dreary" writer
50 Veneration
53 Numbskull
57 No. on a baseball card
59 Gary Cooper film of 1928
61 Overwrought writing
64 Architect I. M. ___
65 Removes, as a knot
66 Sporting sword
67 Nest item
68 Turns back to zero
69 Lifeless
70 "Nope"

DOWN

1 Floaters in northern seas
2 Vigilant
3 Tiny pond plants
4 Aptitude
5 Pizazz
6 Variety show
7 Swim competitions
8 Said "I do" together
9 Norma ___, Sally Field role
10 On the wrong course
11 Paleolithic hammer or ax
12 Skinny
13 Realtor's aim
19 President's foreign policy grp.
21 Light refractor
25 All's opposite
27 Rebuffs rudely
28 Robust
29 E pluribus ___
30 Upside-down sleepers
31 Org. offering creature comforts?
32 Trudge
33 Fenders, taillights, etc.
35 Swelling reducer
36 Where a telescope is aimed
37 "Get it?"
40 Lug
41 Train stop
46 Baked entree with a crust
48 Controlled the mike
50 Austrian peak
51 Sent by bank transfer
52 Get hitched hastily
54 Turn red, as an apple
55 End of the Greek alphabet
56 Whinny
57 Cowboy boot part
58 Ditty
60 Between ports
62 Permit
63 Twisty turn

by Lynn Lempel

ACROSS

1 "Mutiny on the Bounty" captain
6 Half a McDonald's logo
10 Blend
14 Anouk of "La Dolce Vita"
15 Mineral in transparent sheets
16 "Told you I could do it!"
17 1944 Judy Garland movie
20 Feathery scarves
21 Magazine revenue source
22 Soda can opener
23 Gets on the nerves of
25 Mideast leaders
27 Marsh plant
29 Facing trouble
33 With 45-Across, 1993 Tom Hanks/Meg Ryan movie
37 Aerosol
38 Krazy ___ of the comics
39 Jamboree participant
41 Going way back, as friends
42 Dog collar attachment
45 See 33-Across
48 Hits the roof
50 Morales of "NYPD Blue"
51 Pointed, as a gun
53 Mild aftershock
57 "Oh my heavens!"
60 Luau instrument, informally
62 Nickelodeon's ___ the Explorer
63 2000 Richard Gere/Winona Ryder movie

66 Russia's ___ Mountains
67 Early Bond foe
68 Spine-chilling
69 Portend
70 Twist, as findings
71 Utopias

DOWN

1 "La ___," 1959 hit
2 Rest atop
3 "To put it another way . . ."
4 Become peeved
5 Skirt edge
6 Surrounded by
7 Step after shampooing
8 Syringe amts.
9 Millinery accessory
10 Clogs, as a drain

11 Drawn tight
12 Prefix with -syncratic
13 Hoarse voice
18 Flip chart holders
19 The ___ Prayer
24 "You betcha!"
26 Apply incorrectly
28 Make up one's mind
30 Gait between walk and canter
31 Ring up
32 Jekyll's bad side
33 Slaloms
34 Stow, as cargo
35 Suffix with cigar
36 Prince, to a king
40 Exam taker
43 Generally speaking
44 Brother with a fairy tale

46 Swiss river to the Rhine
47 Like some Grateful Dead fans' attire
49 Corrects
52 Irene of "I Remember Mama"
54 Poet Clement C. ___
55 Sen. Hatch
56 Does fall yard work
57 Apply carelessly, as paint
58 Continental coin
59 Not much
61 Have down pat
64 Vex
65 Minuscule

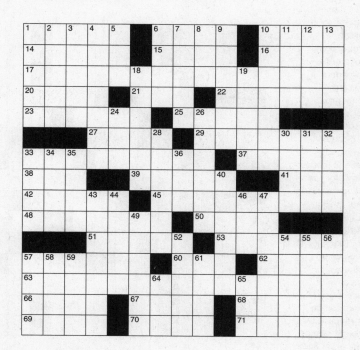

by Harvey Estes

64

ACROSS

1 The life of Riley
5 Blessings
10 "How about ___?!"
14 Voting group
15 AM/FM device
16 Rabbit moves
17 When one might wear a hat
19 Singer India.___
20 Binary code digit
21 Presidential advisers
23 Done permanently, as writing
26 The first "T" of TNT
28 Smart ___ (wiseacres)
29 Neighbor of Vietnam
30 Gidget player in "Gidget"
32 "___ Abner"
33 Popular soap
35 Son of, in Arabic names
36 Motto of New Hampshire
41 Western treaty grp.
42 Rick's love in "Casablanca"
43 Bit of hair cream, say
45 Generic modeling "clay" for tots
49 Bull in a bullfight
50 Airs, in Latin
51 ___ Beta Kappa
52 "A right ___ old elf" (Santa)
53 Three-letter combo
55 Mooer
56 Ascent
57 Stamp on an envelope without enough stamps
63 Verb type: Abbr.
64 ___ Park, Colo.
65 Late civil rights activist Parks
66 "What ___!" ("How cool!")
67 Fashion
68 Headliner

DOWN

1 Flow's partner
2 Chicken ___ king
3 Lawn makeup
4 Sounds in an empty hall
5 Cheese from France
6 Boater's blade
7 Like 1, 3, 5, 7 . . .
8 An essential vitamin
9 Kind of bean
10 It was once Siam
11 Like bulls' heads
12 Each
13 Sleeping sickness carrier
18 Raggedy ___
22 Singer Streisand
23 Running a temperature, say
24 Hammer's target
25 ___ sci (college major, informally)
26 Pre-1917 Russian ruler
27 North Carolina's capital
31 "Vaya con ___" ("Go with God")
33 More tired
34 Assuming that's true
37 Travelers
38 Relating to grades 1–12
39 British rocker Billy
40 Countess's husband
44 "Whew!"
45 Homeland, to Horace
46 Tempting
47 Record label for many rappers
48 Highest
49 TV transmission sites
52 Morning run, perhaps
54 "Planet of the ___"
55 24 cans of beer
58 Hog haven
59 No. with an area code
60 Period
61 Land north of Mex.
62 End point for an iPod cord

by Sarah Keller

ACROSS
1 With: Fr.
5 Milkshake item
10 In ___ (together)
14 Hawaiian port
15 "The Devil Wears ___"
16 Get better, as a cut
17 State with conviction
18 Drive away
19 Artist Bonheur
20 Historic Boston neighborhood
22 Wiggle room
24 Loads and loads
25 Gush
26 Totaling
29 Comedian who created the character Jose Jimenez
33 Manipulate
34 Burden of proof
35 Half a sch. year
36 Toll unit on a toll road
37 What "yo mama" is
39 Cover for a wound
40 Plop oneself down
41 "Are you ___ out?"
42 Gem of an oyster
43 Ailment that may cause sneezing
45 Go by, as time
46 Wolf's sound
47 Jump named for a skater
48 Empty, as a lot
51 Auxiliary wager
55 Composer Stravinsky
56 Some Apples
59 Say yea or nay
60 Line of stitches
61 Modern assembly line worker

62 Love god
63 "The Thin Man" dog
64 Les ___-Unis
65 Mardi Gras follower

DOWN
1 Melville captain
2 Start of a Spanish cheer
3 Util. bill
4 Sound-absorbing flooring
5 Helped bust out, as from prison
6 Cards above deuces
7 Séance sound
8 Juice drink
9 Where to get juice for a household appliance

10 Astute
11 "Man, that hurts!"
12 Astronaut's insignia
13 Potter's medium
21 007
23 Slithery fishes
25 Ireland's ___ Fein
26 Covered with water
27 The South
28 River mouth feature
29 Word that can follow the first words of 20-, 29-, 43- and 51-Across and 4-, 9-, 37- and 39-Down
30 B.M.I. rival
31 Draws nigh
32 Mosey (along)

37 Winter traction provider
38 Lounge
39 Death Valley is below it
41 Computer image
42 Appealed earnestly
44 Greg's sitcom partner
45 Is
47 English race place
48 Document checked at a border
49 Matures
50 Jacket
52 Bloviator, often
53 Princely prep school
54 Exam
57 Bon ___ (witticism)
58 Lawyer's org.

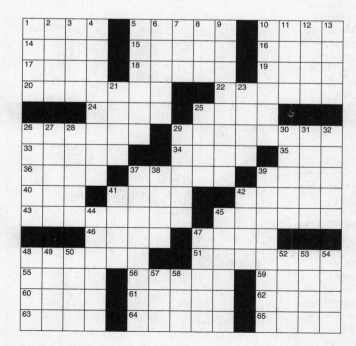

by Paula Gamache

66

ACROSS

1 End place for many a car accident
6 Mire
9 "Shhh!"
14 Novelist Calvino
15 Bother
16 The "U" of UHF
17 Astronaut's attire
18 Fluffy scarf
19 Go into
20 Not the real Charlie of Star-Kist ads?
23 Born: Fr.
24 Big part of an elephant
25 Ambulance worker, for short
26 Tetley product
29 Vintage French wines?
32 Rabble-rouse
34 Inexperienced in
35 Italian volcano
36 Assistant in a con game
39 Nix by Nixon, e.g.
40 Mire
42 Peanuts
44 1960s sitcom ghoul on the terrace?
47 1976 and 2001, e.g.: Abbr.
48 Sunbather's shade
49 Founded: Abbr.
50 Korean automaker
53 What 20-, 29-, 44- and 53-Across are of each other
56 Actress Sarandon
59 "Exodus" hero
60 Muscat native
61 Prank
62 Lower, as the lights
63 Stirred up
64 With feigned shyness
65 Reverse of WNW
66 Trap

DOWN

1 "Start eating!"
2 Reply to "Who's there?"
3 Brownish gray
4 Annual award named for a Muse
5 Stressful spot
6 The Sultan of Swat
7 Smell
8 Uncle Sam facial feature
9 Director Tarantino
10 Arm bone
11 Major defense contractor
12 "But I heard him exclaim, ___ he . . ."
13 Driveway surface
21 Bye-byes
22 Referee
26 Pisa landmark
27 French political divisions
28 Regarding
29 City on Biscayne Bay
30 Have the throne
31 Emphatic no
32 In armed conflict
33 Pesky swarm
35 Catch sight of
37 Lollygag
38 "___ luck!"
41 Effectiveness
43 Racetrack habitués
45 Deface
46 Like beds before housekeeping
50 Australian "bear"
51 Word before tube or circle
52 Off the direct course
53 Bucket
54 "Exodus" author
55 Poker player's declaration
56 Anatomical pouch
57 Tres – dos
58 Muddy enclosure

by John Calvin Williams

ACROSS

1 Soaking site
5 Cry like a baby
9 Early Peruvian
13 Jai ___
14 Category
15 Sweetheart
16 Window ledge
17 Jason's sorceress wife
18 Long and lean
19 Comment upon bumping into an old friend, #1
22 Russian refusal
23 Soul singer James
24 San Francisco/Oakland separator
27 Comment #2
31 John, Paul and George: Abbr.
34 Hi-___ monitor
35 Wordsworth works
36 Pistol, e.g.
39 "Forget about it!"
41 Bubbling on the stove
42 Like sushi
43 Militant '60s campus org.
44 Comment #3
49 Absorb, with "up"
50 Word that's an example of itself
51 Klutz's cry
54 Comment #4
59 "Let's get crackin'!"
61 Forearm bones
62 "Agreed!"
63 Wolf's cry
64 ___ Rizzo of "Midnight Cowboy"
65 Peaceful period
66 ___-bitsy
67 Deuces
68 Häagen-Dazs alternative

DOWN

1 Wingding
2 Visitor from another planet
3 Running total
4 Jewish campus group
5 Borscht ingredient
6 Julie who played Mary Poppins
7 Christmas garland
8 Makeshift shelter
9 Run in place
10 Not-so-potent potables
11 Campbell's container
12 Biblical boat
14 Baseball bigwigs: Abbr.
20 Plains Indian
21 Responses of shock
25 Carrying a weapon
26 Go-aheads
28 Sch. named for a televangelist
29 Author Kesey
30 ___ polloi
31 Persian potentates
32 Just not done
33 Blizzard battlers
37 Opposite of multiplication: Abbr.
38 First American to orbit Earth
39 Arrest
40 Have bills
42 Meet unexpectedly
45 Dannon product
46 Wanted felon
47 Ages and ages
48 Pasta bit
52 Nom de plume: Abbr.
53 Serta competitor
55 Nothing but
56 The "m" of $E = mc^2$
57 "___ Beso" (Paul Anka song)
58 Building additions
59 "The Sweetheart of Sigma ___"
60 Bon ___ (witticism)

by Nancy Salomon

68

ACROSS

1 PC alternatives
5 Big name in pest control
10 Resident of 29-Down
14 "Shake ___" (1981 song by the Cars)
15 "Me, too!"
16 Get the wrinkles out of
17 Dickens's "little" girl
18 Showed interest in, as at a bar
19 This, in Madrid
20 Jakarta
23 Poet's Muse
24 Common Web site section, for short
25 O, Us or GQ
28 Cats' prey
32 TWA competitor
34 "___ Poetica"
37 Nickname for Namath
40 Certain carpet or hairdo
42 Skylit courts
43 What a casting director tries to fill
44 Employee benefit
47 Free from, with "of"
48 Madison Avenue worker
49 Japanese wrestling
50 Take care of a bill
51 Helpers for profs
54 Singer ___ Khan
59 Fuddy-duddy
64 Sites of monkey business?
66 Closet wood
67 Calf-length skirt
68 Rick's love in "Casablanca"
69 Squiggly mark in "señor"
70 Nuclear energy source

71 Peelable fruit
72 Proceed on tiptoe
73 Nasdaq alternative

DOWN

1 Cut into tiny bits
2 "Don't shed ___"
3 "Mea ___"
4 Challenging bowling pin arrangement
5 Agency with workplace regs.
6 Agitate
7 The Green Hornet's valet
8 Cry at a leave-taking
9 "Teenage Mutant ___ Turtles"
10 Chicken ___
11 Big Dipper's locale
12 Decompose
13 Genetic stuff
21 ___ of the Unknowns
22 Blue hue
26 Garlicky mayonnaise
27 King Midas's downfall
29 Mideast land
30 Big maker of perfumes
31 Famous family of Western lawmen
33 Damascus's land: Abbr.
34 B.M.I. rival
35 "The Mary Tyler Moore Show" spinoff
36 1998 National League M.V.P.

38 God, in Paris
39 In the 70's or so
41 3.5, e.g., for a student
45 Prefix with lock
46 1970s–'80s Big Apple mayor
52 Bank holdings: Abbr.
53 Coil of yarn
55 Muscly fellow
56 Friendship
57 Praise
58 Stop on ___
60 Ivan the Terrible, e.g.
61 Not in use
62 It means nothing to Juan
63 Long, long walk
64 12345, in Schenectady, N.Y.
65 Corrida shout

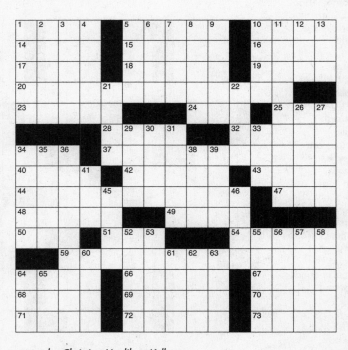

by Christina Houlihan Kelly

ACROSS

1 Practice boxing
5 Setting for "Hansel and Gretel"
10 Like very early education, for short
14 Brand of blocks
15 ___ Hoffman of the Chicago Seven
16 Education by memorization
17 Region
18 Religious belief
19 Super-duper
20 One-L lama
23 Rational
24 "___ Misérables"
25 Cutting up, as logs
28 Housekeeper
30 Crow's call
33 "___ goeth before a fall"
34 Building with a loft
35 Sulk
36 Two-L llama
39 Architect ___ van der Rohe
40 Some Keats poems
41 Put into law
42 Upper chamber member: Abbr.
43 War god on Olympus
44 Speakers' spots
45 No. of ft. above sea level
46 . . . .
47 Three-L lllama?
55 Toward the rising sun
56 Ricochet
57 4, on a sundial
58 Nick at ___
59 Express a thought
60 Lease

61 ___ the Red
62 Stuffed
63 Actions on heartstrings and pant legs

DOWN

1 Hunk of marble, e.g.
2 Where Lima is
3 Elderly
4 Locales for rest stops
5 Using the kiddie pool, say
6 More than fat
7 Sad news item
8 Gossip, slangily
9 Wheat product used in making pasta
10 Bows one's head in church

11 Kitchen or bath
12 Sicilian spouter
13 Eager
21 Fruit of the Loom competitor
22 Conducted
25 Bombards with unwanted e-mail
26 Golfer Palmer, to pals
27 Expand, as a highway
28 Old battle clubs
29 Torah holders
30 Unconscious states
31 Quickly
32 Whip marks
34 Wished
35 Attire covering little of the legs
37 Temple entrances

38 "Groovy!"
43 Drink often labeled XXX in the comics
44 Heading to a bad end
45 Indian conquered by the conquistadors
46 Hum
47 The "B" of N.B.
48 Hideout
49 ___ Spumante (wine)
50 Auto parts giant
51 Londoner, e.g., informally
52 In ___ of (replacing)
53 ___ Yang Twins (rap duo)
54 Things to pick

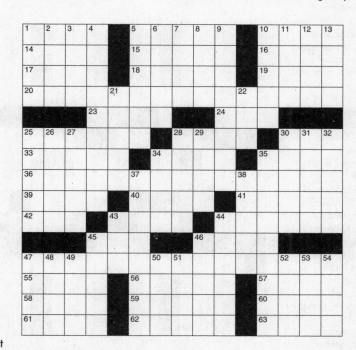

by Peter A. Collins

70

ACROSS

1 Rock outcropping
5 Dive among coral reefs, say
10 Sheep cries
14 Gossipy Barrett
15 Artist's stand
16 Break in the action
17 Wading bird
18 Tear away (from)
19 Airport for Air France
20 FLOP
23 Power for Robert Fulton
24 Razor sharpener
25 Stare (at)
28 Smother
32 Serving of corn
35 Civil rights org.
38 Game move
39 FLAP
43 Kind of lily
44 Royal headpiece
45 Tues. follower
46 Texas city named for a city in Ukraine
49 Keep ___ on (watch)
51 Continental money
54 Marina sights
58 FLIP
62 Pseudonym of H. H. Munro
63 Borden cow
64 Ivy, for one
65 Landed (on)
66 Wasps' homes
67 Part that's sharp
68 ___ club (singers' group)
69 Lovers' get-together
70 Burn the outside of

DOWN

1 Baby holders
2 Mechanical man
3 Japanese cartoon art
4 One who talks, talks, talks
5 In stitches
6 Low-___ diet
7 People before rehab
8 Intoxicate
9 Places for wedding vows
10 Tube on a welding tool
11 Special glow
12 Friend in war
13 Foxlike
21 Native of Muscat
22 "i" topper
26 Washed-out in complexion
27 Actor William of "The Greatest American Hero"
29 Piloted
30 Spend half the afternoon in a hammock, e.g.
31 Got a good look at
32 Exxon, formerly
33 Wowed
34 Fury
36 Greek X
37 Fuel from a bog
40 California national park
41 Victoria's Secret item
42 Jewish leader
47 Take to court
48 Hot-blooded
50 Does crosswords, say
52 Ship from the Mideast
53 Impudent
55 Off the direct path
56 South Seas kingdom
57 Look with a twisted lip
58 Ring up
59 Dust Bowl refugee
60 Tiny complaints
61 Toward sunset
62 Droop

by Bernice Gordon

ACROSS

1 Family
5 Winter neckwear
10 Conclusions
14 Harvard rival
15 ___ Slobbovia (remote locale)
16 Vista
17 Store safely
18 Cockamamie
19 Ancient Peruvian
20 Start of a quote by Bertrand Russell relevant to crossword solvers
23 Roy Orbison's "___ the Lonely"
24 Rots
25 How to divide things to be fair
28 Revolutionary pamphleteer Thomas
30 Supersmart grp.
31 Atmosphere
32 Back talk
36 Ltd.
37 Middle of the quote
40 Chairman with a Little Red Book
41 In ___ of (standing in for)
43 Actor Tim of "WKRP in Cincinnati"
44 Adhesive
46 Pie nut
48 Quenches
49 Simoleons
52 Swizzle
53 Conclusion of the quote
59 Mission-to-Mars org.
60 Cognizant
61 One with adoring fans
62 Squeezed (out)
63 Hayseed

64 Capone fighter Eliot ___
65 Cry from Charlie Brown
66 Pivots
67 Way to get out of a field

DOWN

1 Anatomical sac
2 Strip of wood in homebuilding
3 ___ vera
4 Eponymous units of force
5 By a narrow margin
6 Brooklyn's ___ Island
7 Not at home
8 Gambling mecca
9 Revealing kind of slip
10 Demonstrates clearly
11 Old Japanese assassin
12 Wooden duck, say
13 Persuades
21 Member of an extended family
22 Poetic time after dusk
25 Disney's "___ and the Detectives"
26 "___, vidi, vici" (Caesar's boast)
27 Suffix with differ
28 Vladimir of the Kremlin
29 Like most of west Texas
31 Between ports
33 One way to run
34 ___-Coburg (part of historic Germany)

35 High-protein beans
38 Sites for grand entrances
39 Icy cold
42 Transfers files to a computer, maybe
45 It's "such sweet sorrow"
47 Have supper
48 Braces (oneself)
49 Worker with a light and a pick
50 Japanese port
51 Beginning
52 Spread, as seed
54 Dicey G.I. status
55 Drink with sushi
56 Notion
57 Maximum
58 ". . . or ___!" (threat)

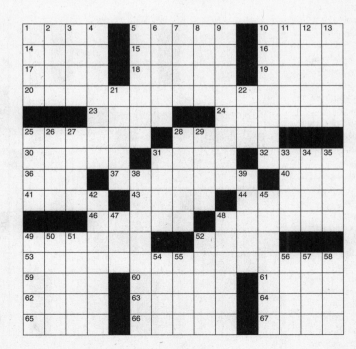

by Marlon R. Howell

ACROSS

1 Variety of poker
5 Actress Rowlands
9 Vice president Spiro
14 Prefix with glycemic
15 Patron saint of Norway
16 Dog's restraint
17 Unlock
18 Not all
19 "Heavens to ___!"
20 "Sahara" co-star, 2005
23 Capital of New Mexico
24 Lagasse of the Food Network, once
28 Shack
29 Up to, briefly
31 Prefix with tiller
32 Luggage attachment
35 Theme
37 Ukraine, e.g., once: Abbr.
38 Trip to Tahiti, for example
41 What andirons support
42 Blocked from sunlight
43 Result of a hit by a leadoff batter
44 Med. school subject
46 "Pick a card, ___ card"
47 Getting on in years
48 Shooting star
50 Italian city on the Adriatic
54 Groups collecting litter
57 Ones attracted to flames
60 ___ Hashanah
61 Landed (on)
62 Sharpshooter Oakley
63 "Puppy Love" singer Paul
64 Heredity unit
65 All gone, as food
66 Ship's petty officer, informally
67 To be: Lat.

DOWN

1 Mall units
2 Aggressive, as a personality
3 Ivy League school in Phila.
4 Words after "been there"
5 Become lenient (on)
6 Act on a sudden itching for a hitching
7 Title
8 With: Fr.
9 Photo book
10 Codger
11 Singer ___ King Cole
12 Letter before tee
13 Philosopher's question
21 Guffaws
22 Archaeological find
25 O'Donnell formerly of "The View"
26 "___ easy to fall in love" (1977 lyric)
27 Sophia of "Two Women"
29 Fawner
30 ___-bitsy
32 Muhammad's religion
33 "Lorna ___"
34 Gently pull on
35 Average
36 Merry play
39 Stock unit
40 20 or less, at a bar
45 Computer whiz
47 Parentless child
49 With 52-Down, showbiz's Mary-Kate and Ashley
50 Walrus features
51 Tennis's Monica
52 See 49-Down
53 Cosmetician Lauder
55 Syrian or Yemeni
56 Taboo
57 Sex kitten West
58 Go ___ rampage
59 Explosive letters

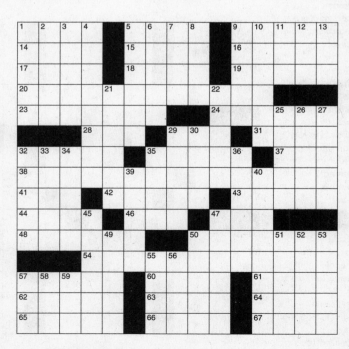

by Richard Chisholm

ACROSS

1 Network to keep an "eye" on
4 Singer's sound
9 Provide for free, informally
13 Sedan or wagon
15 Ancient Peruvians
16 W.W. II general Bradley
17 "___, crackle, pop"
18 Birthplace of 59-Across
20 59-Across, e.g.
22 Having a ghost
23 Cut, as sheep's wool
24 Drunkards
25 TV program for which 59-Across won an Emmy, 1977
32 Debussy's "La ___"
34 Bullfighter's cloth
35 Melodic subject, in music
36 Album for which 59-Across won a Grammy, 1972, with "The"
41 It's a butter alternative
42 "The Wizard of Oz" pooch
43 French word before and after "à"
44 Movie for which 59-Across won an Oscar, 1961
49 The "E" in E.R.: Abbr.
50 Spicy sauce . . . or dance
53 Milan opera house
57 Play for which 59-Across won a Tony, 1975
59 Star born on 12/11/1931
61 ___ the kill

62 Lyric poems
63 Part of the head that may be congested
64 Campbell of the "Scream" movies
65 Snoozes
66 Exams
67 Jiffy

DOWN

1 Spanish houses
2 Cluster
3 Ohio's buckeye, California's redwood, etc.
4 Big shots, for short
5 Burden
6 Freezer trayful
7 Server at a drive-in
8 Aristocrat's home
9 ___ flakes
10 Forget to mention

11 Protective spray
12 Motivate
14 TV host with a book club
19 Get rid of
21 Straight up
24 Phantom
26 Scratch
27 Reuters competitor
28 Engine additive brand
29 Map borders, usually
30 Prefix with potent
31 ___ and Means Committee
32 Tabby's cry
33 French "she"
37 Foldaway bed
38 Comedian Bill, informally
39 Giant slugger Mel
40 Antlered animal

45 Tailor's line
46 "This is not making sense to me"
47 Little loved one
48 ___ to go (eager)
51 Ward (off)
52 Pre-Columbus Mexican
53 Scientologist ___ Hubbard
54 Opera set in the age of pharaohs
55 Stair part
56 Mama ___ of the Mamas and the Papas
57 Carpenter's metal piece
58 "Bonanza" brother
60 Lt.'s inferior, in the Navy

by David J. Kahn

ACROSS

1 Cry after "Forward!"
6 Solder
10 Belgrade native
14 Central Florida city
15 Words of understanding
16 Peter, Paul and Mary, e.g.
17 Holiday decoration
20 Retain
21 Numbered work of a composer
22 "Come in!"
23 Preservers of preserves
25 "This looks bad!"
27 Cleopatra's lover
30 Hissy fit
31 Air blower
34 Like a pitcher's perfect game
35 Flub
36 Look into a crystal ball
37 Holiday decoration
40 Fabric fuzz
41 Memo opener
42 Plural of 21-Across
43 U-turn from WSW
44 Assns.
45 Frigate or ferry
46 Fleeting trace
47 Neat
48 Offspring
51 Butcher's cut
53 Shopping place
57 Holiday decoration
60 Abbr. before a colon
61 Feed the kitty
62 Make amends
63 General emotional state
64 Some boxing decisions, briefly
65 Snapshot

DOWN

1 Make fun of
2 Liniment target
3 Like one in a million
4 Business that routinely overcharges
5 Possesses
6 Ones likely to chicken out
7 Biblical pottage purchaser
8 First chapter in a primer
9 Morning moisture
10 Shorthand pro
11 The "E" in Q.E.D.
12 Baptism or bar mitzvah
13 Danish Nobelist Niels
18 British Conservative
19 What homeowners don't have to pay
24 1998 animated bug film
26 Player of 45's
27 Site for a monitoring bracelet, maybe
28 Hopeless, as a situation
29 Feudal landholder
30 Whiskey drinks
31 Confronts
32 Sky-blue
33 View from Mount Everest
35 Ship-to-shore accessway
36 Insect whose larvae destroy foliage
38 Broadcasts
39 ___ the line (behaved)
44 Pig's sound
45 Handful for Tarzan
46 Coiled
47 Multiplied by
48 Pillow cover
49 Famed Roman censor
50 Diggin'
52 "___ be in England": Browning
54 Suffix with buck
55 Long, angry discourse
56 Lt. Kojak
58 Krazy ___ of the comics
59 Doze

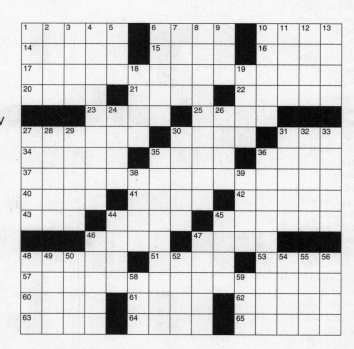

by Donna Levin

ACROSS

1 Up to the task
5 Machinist's tool
10 Study all night, say
14 Common cause of postponement
15 Rural units
16 Olympic swimmer's assignment
17 Regis Philbin and others
20 Hive occupant
21 Ariz. neighbor
22 Actor Milo
23 Actress Farrow
24 Foal's mother
26 Motion picture academy honor
33 Tureen accessory
34 Hands (out)
35 Wall St. deal
36 Mystery writer ___ Stanley Gardner
37 "See? . . . huh, huh?"
38 Emptiness
39 Get older
40 Gift recipient
41 Lemon peels, e.g.
42 Alumni
45 Toward shelter
46 Passé
47 Beauty's counterpart
50 The Beatles, e.g.
52 ___ Na Na
55 There's one in 17-, 26- and 42-Across
59 Gen. Robert ___
60 Alaskan native
61 Transnational currency
62 Wines to serve with beef
63 Singer Turner and others
64 Comic Sandler

DOWN

1 ___-Israeli relations
2 Sweetie pie
3 Head case?
4 Finale
5 Nonprofessional
6 Part of a French play
7 Cereal "for kids"
8 Haw's partner
9 Language suffix
10 Place for hangers
11 Impetuous
12 A few chips, say, in poker
13 Tableland
18 Japanese cartoon style
19 Jewish circle dances
23 French miss: Abbr.
24 Setting
25 Working without ___
26 North Dakota's largest city
27 Slacker
28 Danish birthplace of Hans Christian Andersen
29 Sacred choral work
30 Irving Berlin's "When ___ You"
31 Back-of-newspaper section
32 Nonverbal O.K.'s
33 Bit of foliage
37 Reason for an R rating
38 Sell
40 Airline once said to be "ready when you are"
41 Nintendo's The Legend of ___
43 Pulverizes
44 Dunkable treats
47 1930s boxing champ Max
48 Vogue competitor
49 Mimicked
50 Square in the first column of bingo
51 Water
52 Simple earring
53 Zeus' wife
54 Molecule part
56 Flier in a cave
57 ___ Lilly, maker of Prozac
58 Actor Stephen of "The Crying Game"

by Adam G. Perl

The New York Times

CROSSWORDS

SMART PUZZLES PRESENTED WITH STYLE

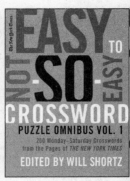

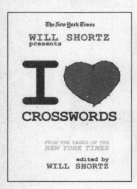

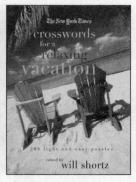

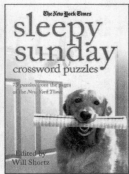

Available at your local bookstore or online at nytimes.com/nytstore.

St. Martin's Griffin

1

```
O N C E   I D E A L   F A S T
L E I A   R E T R O   O N T O
D O N T B E A S T R A N G E R
    M U D D   E N D Z O N E
P A V E S   E S S E S   L O U
A T E   B N A I   R A S P
C A E S A R   R A D I O
  D R O P I N A N Y T I M E
  L T C O L   A O L E R S
L O G O   B E I N   N A P
A L A   T I L E S   B O S S Y
W E L F A R E   O D I N
Y A L L C O M E B A C K N O W
E R O O   N A V A L   E A R P
R Y N E   S N A R E   Y M C A
```

2

```
O B I T   H E C H E   D R A B
W I F I   E C L A T   R E P O
N O S E A R O U N D   A C R O
    T B O N E     T W A I N
S M E A R   O D D C O U P L E
T A L C U M   E A R P
E D S   P A C M A N   O F F
P A I N T T H E T O W N R E D
T E E   Z I T H E R   I D O
    T O O L   D I C T U M
S N O W W H I T E   T R O P E
M U R A L   O M A H A
I D I G   J O B O P E N I N G
L I N E   I R A T E   N C A A
E E G S   M E T E D   Y E G G
```

3

```
B O B U P   F L U B   G E A R
A B A S E   I O T A   O M N I
L I B E R A L B E N E F I T S
K E Y   F L I E S   V E R S E
    L E I A   P E R
R A D I C A L S I G N   A L T
A L E R T S   M E A T S T E W
I L I A   O A R   L A N A
N O T S O F A R   P O U R I N
S T Y   L E F T H A N G I N G
    A D Z   A Y E S
S T Y L E   P A T T Y   H A T
P R O G R E S S I V E L E N S
I O W A   L A I N   A O R T A
N Y S E   S T A G   R Y D E R
```

4

```
P O P S   C O A S T   H A L F
A N E W   A L L A H   O L I O
S T R I P T E A S E   M E S A
T O U P E E   S H E   E X A M
      E A R L   N R A
S K A   S A N D D O L L A R
C I T E D   R E O   B O O Z E
A T A L E   E G G   I N C U R
M E R I T   D E L   N E H R U
P R I M E M O V E R   S E N
    I R A   G O B S
W O O D   G O T   T A P O U T
A L V A   P A I N T H O R S E
S E A T   I R E N E   T E S S
H O L E   E S S E N   S O R T
```

5

```
M A R I E   A D D S   A C T
A M A N D A   N U D E   R H O
T O N S I L   G E T A G R I P
E N G   T E A L     E O N S
  G E T O U T O F T H E W A Y
    E R T E   R E A
U R S A   H E A D G E A R
G E T T H I S S T R A I G H T
H O U S E S A T   R O S E
    L A G   M A S T
G E T A L O A D O F T H A T
A N O N   Y O U R   F U N
G E T A L I F E   S O N A T A
O R E   O V E R   E N A C T S
N O D   B Y E S   G E T I T
```

6

```
F L A G   F O C I   S A L U T
E A R L   R A I N   A L O N E
S P E A K O F T H E D E V I L
S P A D E   Y A P S   E T E
    T E A S   L E O   L E X
S I T O N T H E F E N C E
A S H   S O A P   G O T O N
G L I B   P H O T O   O T T O
A E S O P   C I R C   E I N
  S T A Y T H E C O U R S E
E P I   R O W   R A M P
C O D   T R E E   I S L I P
O B E D I E N C E S C H O O L
L O U I E   T H E E   O C T O
E X P O S   Y O G A   T H A W
```

7

```
E S A U . S O D . A T L A S T
B A N S . C R Y . R O A D I E
B Y G E O R G E . T E N U R E
S A L . Y E A R . . G L E N .
. H E A V E N S T O B E T S Y .
. . B E N . . O L E . . . . .
S A T B Y . G O O D G O L L Y
A T I E . I R A T E . N E M O
O H M Y S T A R S . G E T N O
. . . . I A M . . H I T . . .
W E L L B L O W M E D O W N .
A X E L . . H A R D . H U E
R E V A M P . O H M Y W O R D
T R E M O R . L E A . H O S E
S T E A D Y . E R N . O P E N
```

8

```
S E E P . S C A L A . A C E S
P L E A . P E R I L . F O G G
A L L S H O O K U P . A L O T
. . . S I T S . . H A R I .
H A W K S . P S A T . N A G
A L E E . S T R A T A . P S I
I T S Y . H A I L E D . O T B
R O T S . E L V I S . A W O L
C O G . P L I A N T . P E R U
U N E . E L A T E S . P L I E
T A R . E A S E . . H A L A S
. . M A R C . . A P E R . .
R E A R . K I N G C R E O L E
C O N E . E V E R T . N A I L
A N Y A . D E G A S . T R E K
```

9

```
C R A B . O C T E T . P L O T
H O L A . A R I S E . L E G O
A M O S . F O R C E F I E L D
D A T E L I N E . S L A K E D
. . B O S E . C H A N . .
S P L A S H . S H O W T I M E
L U L L S . S L A T . S O D
O R A L . A I R . S A N G
T E M . H U N T . S P A T E
H E A D L O C K . M E E K E R
. . O I L Y . W A L E . .
P A L T R Y . M A I L D R O P
S P A C E C R A F T . W A K E
A S T O . O A T E R . A C R E
T E E M . W H E R E . Y E A R
```

10

```
A M I N . C R A W . Z A P P A
S A N E . A N N A . A D O R N
F I R S T L A D Y . N O S E D
O N E T O . S A S E . S S E
R E S . S E C O N D G U E S S
. . E D S E L . S I R S . .
A C R E . L U X . E A S E L
C O V E R S E V E R Y B A S E
C R E P E . I D O . L I S A
. . E D I T . E L L E N . .
T H I R D D E G R E E . T S K
O A R . W I N O . D I J O N
G R E T A . H O M E A L O N E
A S N E R . U N I T . S A I L
S H E L F . T Y R A . A N A T
```

11

```
F A N G . A G A T E . E V E R
A R E A . M O T O R . X E N A
A T O Z . O T E R I . I R A N
. A U C T I O N B L O C K
Y U M . G O I N . Y E N T L
I N O I L . . I S T . A S E
P I C N I C H A M P E R .
E S S O . H O S E A . U P A T
. R E A L I T Y C H E C K
S A N . L T D . O R T H O
T R A S H . S O T S . S Y S
A L U M I N U M F O I L .
M E S A . A N I T A . Y E A R
O N E R . M I L E S . N E M O
S E A T . E V E N T . X R A Y
```

12

```
R E A P . E A R S . G L A S S
A X L E . S T E P . A U D I E
Y E A R . C L E A N S L A T E
S C R U B O A K . A L L I E D
. . . I R S . E V A . R D S
H A Z M A T . S W I M S . .
A L O E S . S W E E P H A N D
R O O S . M E A L S . E R I E
D U S T D E V I L . P L A N E
. . A R D E N . R I F L E D
E S P . A I R . N E T . .
A P E R C U . W A S H S A L E
V A C U U M T U B E . A J A X
E T A I L . A S E A . M A G I
S E N N A . P S S T . E R S T
```

13

```
S A S H   C A P O S   B A B A
A R T Y   A N I M E   E N O S
R O O M S T O L E T   A T O P
A S O N E   N O G O   G I N S
N E P A L I   T A N G L E
      L A N A     R E L A X
P U N S   P R E V U E   I S M
E R A   N E C K I N G   T E A
A D S   U N S E A L   P E A S
L U C I D     L I C E
    A C E T I C   T H R A L L
C A R E   A V O W   I G L O O
A L F A   N O V A S C O T I A
S T A G   G R E C O   L A R D
H O N E   S Y N O D   A R E S
```

14

```
S P A M   M A C S   S E G A R
T A D A   A L A W   I R E N E
O N U S   D O M E   C I T G O
W E L C O M E P A C K E T
E L T O R O   R A D   O P S
      T E N N I S R A C K E T
L B J   S E E P   Y E N T L
I O U S   Y E A S T   L O R E
B R I A R   N O A H   W O O
Y E L L O W J A C K E T
A S L   A H A   E R A S E S
    I N C O M E B R A C K E T
C O A C H   M I L O   T O R I
A U R A E   E R O O   I S I N
M I D A S   D E B T   C H E T
```

15

```
P A R E R S   B Y E   C B S
A B I L E N E   O A K T R E E
P O P F O U L   O P E R A T E
E D U   B A L M S   I S A N
R E P E L   N E T   R A H
    S A I D N O   A D D E D
D O C T O R   S W A N   I D O
E R R A T I C   N E S T E G G
A L A   I S L E   R O U T E S
L Y C R A   A P L O M B
    K I N   P E A   S E E M S
B A S S   S T E M S   V I I
A C H E F O R   B I G B A N G
D I O R A M A   S P I E D O N
E D T   R E P   S N E E R S
```

16

```
U M A S S   P L U M S   J A W
T E N T H   H O S E A   U S E
E N D R O A D W O R K   S S E
    A V I S   L E N T E N
W A F T E D   V I I   O M N I
A B R A D E   A N N O T A T E
D U E   S P C A   O R R
S T E P S   L A P   H E R B S
    K E Y   A N T S   I R A
T R I A S S I C   U P B E A T
E A T S   A N Y   S L E D G E
A T T E S T   T H U S
S T E   P R I Z E I N S I D E
E E N   A A R O N   K I L O S
T D S   S P E E D   S E E M S
```

17

```
L E W D   D W A R F   J E S T
A R E A   R A R E R   U T A H
W I N B Y A N O S E   M A U I
N E T   A M E S   E B B I N G
    F A C A D E S   A L L A H
S M I R K S   T U B E
T O R T   R E U S E   U S N
L O S E O N E S B A L A N C E
O T T   C O N E S   A D O S
    N E W T   C A R E T S
S A M O A   S O B E R E R
A L U M N I   C O D A   O U I
V I S A   D R A W A B L A N K
E K E D   O I L E R   E T T E
R E D S   L O A D S   W H O A
```

18

```
M A M M A   A D S   A B U T S
A B E A T   L E T   N E P A L
T E R R A   T A I   T A S T Y
A L V I N T O F F L E R
    N E O   F E N   T L C
S I M O N W I E S E N T H A L
E M O   D I V A   A R O M A
D I O R   T E R M S   I M A M
A G R E E   L O T T   A Z O
T H E O D O R E D R E I S E R
E T D   W W I   E R N
    T H E C H I P M U N K S
A T A R I   H A N   I R E N E
R O G E T   E S T   T E H E E
M O O S E   R H O   E D I E S
```

19

```
CORA  RACK  SHIRE
IHOP  ELLA  PUREE
VAST  BOOB  EMAIL
IRE COTTONCANDY
CAGIER   BEIN
  ATONAL  REESES
PARIS  GOATS  UVA
OLDS  BOWLS  AGES
LIE  RAGES  URALS
KANSAS  ROUTER
  ANTS  PASSUP
ORANGECRUSH  HMO
VERDE  RASH  TABS
INNER  OREO  ACRE
DOORS  DART  OKAY
```

20

```
PULSE  WOLF  TEAK
ANITA  ALAI  ARLO
IDEAS  LESS  XMAS
DOUBTINGTHOMAS
   EDU  EVA
 IMNOTBUYINGIT
HOSED  EKED  ERA
ARUG  MODES  SNOB
ZZZ  LOCO  BURNS
YOUCANTFOOLME
  RBI  NBA
WHOSKIDDINGWHO
CHAW  ESAU  KARAN
COLD  RANT  EVERT
CATS  SWAY  TENTO
```

21

```
APSE  KAYO  SQUAT
SHAM  ONUP  EUROS
TONI  WILE  DANKE
REDLETTERDAY
ABA  BOA  AUK  WIZ
YELLOWSUBMARINE
  INS  SOB  UFOS
MONEY  LUX  EBERT
AGOG  AER  CXI
GREENBAYPACKERS
EEL  ARP  RTE  GEE
 TRAFFICLIGHT
INFER  ROMA  SNIT
QUITO  ORAL  TORE
STREW  GALL  OGEE
```

22

```
ROT  MARCO  AMOR
EVEL  DWELL  LAMA
LANECLOSED  EDEN
ELENA  LEASE  EGG
ESTATE  WRONGWAY
    ELF  DONO
NOPARKING  ARMS
BRADS  BIO  ISSET
CANI  STOPAHEAD
  TEAS  NAG
NOOUTLET  DRYADS
ELM  MIRED  EATIT
SLIM  DONOTENTER
TIME  ESSES  GIGA
SEEN  REESE  COP
```

23

```
GNAT  PRAMS  SLUM
REDO  LAPAT  TENT
REDSNAPPER  OTIS
 DECENT  ABOUT
DINAR  DRPEPPER
OED  FAREAST  ORA
GRAS  REVS  TENSE
  THEGIPPER
CARLA  ASEA  ENID
ACE  PALERMO  ESE
BEBOPPER  ALARM
 TOKYO  SAHARA
GALA  LASTSUPPER
ATTY  LITUP  SALE
MESS  OMENS  ERIC
```

24

```
SSS  STRAP  SCALP
PIC  PHILS  EERIE
ADO  RELEE  ALTER
METROSEXUALS
SATOUT  ADS  APT
  STIR  OPENBAR
SUIT  NUB  TIBIA
UNDERGROUNDFILM
SPORE  GLO  TESS
HOLSTER  THAI
ITS  BEE  AGENDA
 SUBWAYSERIES
KAYAK  ARESO  ELI
ELATE  STALL  CAD
GAMES  HOSED  EYE
```

25

A	S	C	O	T	■	C	U	B	S	■	H	A	S	P
C	H	O	R	E	■	I	S	E	E	■	O	T	T	O
C	A	P	R	A	■	C	O	N	G	E	R	E	E	L
E	L	Y	■	C	O	E	■	T	A	B	■	A	V	A
P	L	E	T	H	O	R	A	■	■	B	A	S	I	N
T	O	D	O	■	H	O	N	D	A	■	N	E	E	D
S	W	I	S	S	■	■	T	E	M	P	T	■	■	■
■	■	T	H	I	N	G	A	M	A	J	I	G	■	■
■	■	I	S	A	A	C	■	■	S	O	R	E	S	■
B	O	M	B	■	T	Y	I	N	G	■	C	O	N	E
O	C	E	A	N	■	■	D	O	N	S	H	U	L	A
I	T	S	■	O	A	K	■	R	U	M	■	N	A	B
L	A	S	T	D	A	N	C	E	■	A	N	D	R	E
E	V	E	S	■	R	E	D	S	■	S	I	E	G	E
D	E	S	K	■	P	E	S	T	■	H	A	R	E	S

26

H	U	T	■	A	T	M	■	■	A	M	B	I	T
O	P	A	L	■	B	R	E	R	■	T	E	A	M	O
M	L	I	I	■	B	O	D	E	■	M	A	D	A	M
B	O	N	D	J	A	M	E	S	B	O	N	D	■	■
R	A	T	S	O	■	P	A	I	L	S	■	R	B	I
E	D	S	■	D	R	E	■	D	O	T	■	E	A	R
■	■	■	P	I	E	■	B	U	T	■	C	A	K	E
■	H	O	M	E	S	W	E	E	T	H	O	M	E	■
R	E	V	S	■	T	I	E	■	E	O	N	■	■	■
E	R	E	■	S	A	L	■	A	R	M	■	A	D	E
P	E	R	■	A	T	L	A	S	■	E	S	S	E	X
■	■	T	I	M	E	A	F	T	E	R	T	I	M	E
S	L	U	R	P	■	R	O	O	M	■	O	D	O	R
A	U	R	A	L	■	D	O	R	M	■	W	E	N	T
S	C	E	N	E	■	■	T	S	A	■	■	S	S	S

27

S	T	O	R	M	■	D	E	N	■	T	I	N	A	S
C	A	R	N	E	■	A	V	E	■	A	N	A	R	T
A	P	A	S	S	A	G	E	T	O	I	N	D	I	A
M	E	L	■	S	C	A	R	■	S	L	E	A	Z	Y
■	■	■	H	A	M	M	■	A	T	E	E	■	■	■
G	A	R	A	G	E	A	T	T	E	N	D	A	N	T
A	D	E	L	E	■	■	W	O	R	D	■	R	O	O
M	O	D	E	■	L	I	E	N	S	■	E	S	T	A
M	R	I	■	F	A	R	E	■	■	D	R	O	I	D
A	N	G	E	L	S	A	N	D	S	A	I	N	T	S
■	■	■	S	O	T	S	■	R	O	M	E	■	■	■
S	A	R	T	R	E	■	Y	O	D	A	■	O	E	R
T	H	E	H	I	D	D	E	N	A	G	E	N	D	A
A	S	P	E	N	■	A	T	E	■	E	L	C	I	D
B	O	O	R	S	■	B	I	D	■	D	I	E	T	S

28

S	P	A	D	E	■	T	H	O	M	■	R	U	E	D
A	R	I	E	L	■	E	U	R	O	■	O	N	M	E
D	I	R	T	F	A	R	M	E	R	■	T	I	M	E
A	D	E	E	■	G	E	E	■	T	I	T	T	E	R
T	E	R	R	I	E	S	■	R	I	C	E	■	■	■
■	■	■	G	R	E	A	S	E	M	O	N	K	E	Y
H	O	M	E	S	■	■	E	D	E	N	■	E	P	A
A	M	E	S	■	A	S	T	O	R	■	S	E	E	P
N	A	N	■	O	M	I	T	■	■	J	O	N	E	S
G	R	U	N	G	E	R	O	C	K	E	R	■	■	■
■	■	■	U	R	N	S	■	R	E	T	R	A	C	T
N	E	S	T	E	A	■	E	E	E	■	E	L	L	A
U	R	A	L	■	M	U	D	S	L	I	N	G	E	R
M	I	L	E	■	E	M	I	T	■	S	T	E	E	D
B	E	E	T	■	N	A	T	S	■	P	O	R	K	Y

29

O	D	D	E	R	■	A	H	A	B	■	H	A	H	A
C	R	O	N	Y	■	T	O	F	U	■	I	M	A	X
C	O	N	T	E	N	T	S	F	R	A	G	I	L	E
U	N	O	■	■	Y	E	T	I	■	S	H	E	L	L
R	E	T	A	K	E	N	■	R	O	A	D	■	■	■
■	■	■	S	K	I	■	D	A	M	P	■	A	T	T	Y
I	N	T	A	N	D	E	M	■	A	N	Y	H	O	O
V	I	A	■	K	E	E	P	D	R	Y	■	I	R	K
E	N	C	A	S	E	■	L	E	T	M	E	S	E	E
S	A	K	E	■	R	T	E	S	■	P	A	S	■	■
■	■	■	R	H	E	A	■	S	C	H	T	I	C	K
A	D	L	A	I	■	T	I	E	R	■	D	O	I	■
P	R	O	T	E	C	T	F	R	O	M	H	E	A	T
T	I	N	E	■	P	O	S	T	■	S	A	U	L	T
S	P	E	D	■	R	O	O	S	■	G	Y	P	S	Y

30

A	D	H	O	C	■	R	A	L	P	H	■	B	L	T
B	Y	A	I	R	■	I	N	U	R	E	■	L	I	E
B	E	L	L	Y	D	A	N	C	E	R	■	O	E	D
E	S	T	■	U	R	L	S	■	A	B	A	C	U	S
■	■	■	A	N	A	T	■	A	C	I	D	■	■	■
■	L	U	C	K	O	F	T	H	E	D	R	A	W	■
N	E	E	D	L	E	■	A	M	Y	■	U	S	A	■
A	R	N	I	E	■	O	K	S	■	B	A	S	I	L
S	I	D	■	E	V	E	■	R	E	L	E	N	T	■
H	E	A	D	O	V	E	R	H	E	E	L	S	■	■
■	■	■	C	H	I	N	■	O	A	F	S	■	■	■
L	O	W	C	A	L	■	E	R	I	C	■	A	D	O
A	L	A	■	R	O	A	S	T	M	A	S	T	E	R
M	E	N	■	A	N	D	S	O	■	K	A	R	M	A
P	O	T	■	S	E	V	E	N	■	E	M	A	I	L

31

```
LUTES  KARL  DEEP
OPERA  OLIO  ECRU
CREATURECOMFORT
KITS  NECKTIE
USE  LEAK  SCRAP
PERSIA  DESTINE
   PERDIEM  MOP
 BEASTOFBURDEN
SEA  HOSTLER
SARCASM  SAYING
SUSAN  PAIR  NOR
  INFERNO  ASIA
ANIMALMAGNETISM
DIVA  AIDS  TOTEM
OXEN  TROT  AMUSE
```

32

```
LATIN  SLIT  SHOD
ATONE  EASE  TONE
VOTER  AILS  ORAL
AMORVINCITOMNIA
   TED  PEPPERY
FAB  DIES  DIS
AWE  OSLO  NOISE
NONCOMPOSMENTIS
GLEAN  NOSE  ALA
  MED  POLS  LOU
AWAITED  OID
PERSONANONGRATA
REDO  IBAR  NAVAL
IDOL  RAZE  ANITA
LYRE  OTIS  LOVER
```

33

```
APSO  OSCAR  RINK
GAUL  FLARE  EDEN
AUDI  FORESTFIRE
SLAV  ORATE  OVA
PINESAP  ACTED
 BUDS  LOSE
ANDREA  DERELICT
RONA  GREEN  ECON
PRANCERS  ABRUPT
 CASS  STAY
SHAHS  PEASOUP
COB  TOTAL  TUNE
AVOCADOPIT  ATTN
LEVI  DISCO  LIII
PLEA  SLEEP  KEEN
```

34

```
ROVER  MOMS  FAZE
ENERO  ALAI  ARID
BARRTENDED  RING
ANY  AMOS  ENRAGE
 STIR  WAIF
CASTOR  CARNEGIE
ALTAR  TRIM  TEMP
BAER  THATS  CASE
OMAR  REFS  THREE
TOMSWIFT  CHESTS
 HAFT  COED
AYEAYE  BOMB  SHE
HARP  CARRPOOLED
ELIE  TRIG  SNARE
MEND  ACTI  SEVEN
```

35

```
DECO  CAPO  GLOW
ENOLA  HOOK  REDO
INDEXCARDS  AMOK
SUE  ERST  AZURE
MIDDLEMANAGERS
 ESE  OTIS
SLAM  IOWAN  UFO
PUTONESFINGERON
AXE  ALLAN  KNEE
 ERLE  EVE
 PINKYTUSCADERO
CEDES  LION  DEG
USER  RINGLEADER
STAG  IRAN  SPIKE
POLY  MESS  TESS
```

36

```
APES  PARCH  SKIS
MOMA  ALCOA  KINK
RUBBERBAND  ANTI
ARRIVE  SIS  NED
DIANE  SOUTHBEND
INC  RAHAL  ERASE
OGEE  YUK  FEARED
 SPELLBIND
PASTAS  ALF  YMCA
ALIEN  SWEEP  COG
JAMESBOND  LUCRE
AMP  YAW  MARLON
MESA  GERMANBUND
ADOS  ETHAN  AREA
SANK  LOOPY  NETS
```

37

```
W A L K   P A W N   S A M B A
I L I E   A C H E   U L E E S
R A C E   P R I X   B I Z E T
E M I L I O E S T E V E Z
D O T   L O S T   M E N A C E
    A S S   S I R   N A M
E X T R A E F F O R T   I R A
A H E M   E C O   A N T I
T O L   E L E C T R I C E E L
U S E   D I D   E T E
P A M P A S   G A P E   P A Y
  E A S T E R N E M P I R E
A S T I N   B A J A   A Q U A
L O R N E   R I O T   T U B S
F L Y E R   O N U S   H E A T
```

38

```
I M A C S   L A G   S C A L A
M O R A L   O V A   C O D E S
S P I N A L T A P   R U R A L
    D Y E S   B E G O N E
A B B Y   V A N N A W H I T E
F L A B B Y   B I N   S T O P
A U R A L   L A N A I
R E D R O S E   O L D S A L T
    C H E S S   E A G E R
A D E S   O Z S   S A Y I D O
B A N K B R A N C H   O N A N
A T T I R E   A E O N
C I R C A   H O L D W A T E R
U V E A S   A L L   E R A S E
S E E P S   Y E S   D A R T S
```

39

```
A L A N   T A D A   E S T E S
S A N E   O L E S   Q U A K E
H U G O B L A C K   U M B E R
E R R   I D S   T E A M U S A
N A Y S A Y   M O N T E
  P L A Z A   D E R I V E
A S S A Y   E R L E   S M E W
M O W N   L A K E R   T U N A
A L A I   A L E G   R O S I N
J E T S K I   T O P I C
  H A N K S   E D K O C H
S E T F R E E   S A G   C H A
E X I L E   M I N C E M E A T
M E L E E   P O O H   C A L E
I S L A M   T C B Y   I N K S
```

40

```
S K I M P   I L L S   F E E D
C A R O L   B E A U   A X L E
A N I M A L M A G N E T I S M
R E S   C A S K   L A T T E S
    H A M   R I T E
V E G E T A B L E G A R D E N
E C O L E   E I G H T   A X E
N O R M   D A V I T   F L A W
O L E   G E T E M   R E A C T
M I N E R A L D E P O S I T S
    M A D E   L S T
S A L I N E   B L U E   B O Y
T W E N T Y Q U E S T I O N S
A O N E   E U R O   T R A C E
G L O M   S I G N   A S T E R
```

41

```
M A R C H   T M A N   A R M S
G L A R E   A U T O   C O A L
R O T O R O O T E R   C L U E
S T E P O N I T   T I L D E
  S I T S   H A N D S E T
T O R   N O T   A F T E R
A D O B E   N R A   N O U N
L I M O   R A N D R   T Y P E
K E P T   I S E   A S C O T
  E T A T S   O W L   E N S
A C R O B A T   R A S P
H A R M S   P A N O R A M A
E R O S   R O U N D R O B I N
A L O U   R U N G   A T E S T
D A M P   S I T E   N O L T E
```

42

```
S U B S   S L I D   S T A M P
O G R E   T E R I   N E P A L
F L A T B R O K E   E M O T E
T I S S U E   S T R A P P E D
    S T E M   O D E
N C A A   T A P A S   R A V E
A U D I O   R A D I O   N I T
F E E L I N G T H E P I N C H
T I P   L O O I E   E V I A N
A N T S   S T O R M   E E R O
    P H I   E A C H
I N T H E R E D   P E A R L S
H O S E R   T A P P E D O U T
O P A R T   C R E E   I O T A
P E R E Z   H E R D   T M E N
```

43

```
A D A M S . H A M S . M R E D
R E N E W . O M A N . Y O Y O
M A N N A . F A T E . B O R N
. L A D Y O F T H E L A K E .
. . B R A . . . Z E D . . . .
M A C R A E . D I E D . P G A
E T H I C . S O F A . N O R M
C H I C K E N O F T H E S E A
C O M E . T O N Y . E A S E S
A S P . H O W E . C A T E R S
. . E M U . . . B E D . . . .
. G E M O F T H E O C E A N .
N O R A . F O A L . A R I E S
A N T I . E A R L . S O L V E
P E E L . E D D Y . E S S E X
```

44

```
S C A T . A D A M S . A C H E
H A R E . R E B U T . S H O T
I R O N . E L E N A . P A T S
P A S S F A I L C L A S S . .
S T E E R . H E S . E S S .
. . S E P I A . . S W A T H
A G A . Y E S N O A N S W E R
T U T U . T A T A R . W A V E
O N O F F S W I T C H . Y E W
M I N O R . C H O I R . . . .
S T E . A L E . R O L E S
. T R U E F A L S E T E S T
C L I O . A L L A H . A P S O
H A M S . F A T S O . T E E N
E Y E S . S T A T E . E R N E
```

45

```
C A R A T S . C H E . C R A B
O N E C U P . H A L . L A N A
S T U C C O W A L L . A M E N
A S P . S T I F F A R M I N G
. . F O S S E . O U S T S .
J A S O N . . C O O P . . .
A L I E . S P E E D S . G U Y
W O R S E C O N D I T I O N S
S T E . G O T T E N . R I D E
. . C A T S . D O N O R .
S W O R D . A S P E N .
T I M E S T A B L E S . F A A
E L I A . B E F O R E H A N D
A C T S . A R A . E R M I N E
D O S E . R O B . S T O R E S
```

46

```
H A S P S . N O C A L . D A M
A L L A H . A L I C E . R I O
N U I S A N C E T A X . A M O
A M P S . O R G . D I G G E R
. P A T E . S E C U R E S
L U P O N E . R A M O N A .
O P A R T . S E V E N . C O W
E D I T . N A M E S . P I N E
B O N . S A L E S . P O N C E
. K I T K A T . B U L G E D
A N I S E E D . R O P E .
M A L T E D . A I L . S A N G
W I L . P E S T C O N T R O L
A V E . E Y D I E . R A I S E
Y E R . N E S T S . A R D E N
```

47

```
W A R D . R I F E . F A R C E
I L I E . E A R N . A B U Z Z
F U N F I L L E D . C E S A R
I M G A M E . E T C E T E R A
. . C P A . D O F F . . .
A C H E . S A O . C A S I N G
B R O . F E M M E . C U R I O
F A N T A S Y F O O T B A L L
A N D E S . S I N U S . Q E D
B E A T T Y . G S T . P I S A
. . F I S H . V I A . . .
S T E P O N I T . O N C A L L
M A R I O . F E E T F I R S T
U P E N D . T R U E . N E A R
T E S T S . S S R S . O A T S
```

48

```
S C A M . N O R M . P L U T O
H A R E . A L O E . R A V E N
E R I C . M A T A . O P E R A
B L A C K E Y E D S U S A N .
A S S A I L . O R D . . .
. S W E E T W I L L I A M
H O N . I S T O . Y U C C A
A L O T . S A Y A H . G O N G
D I A N A . O R A L . N E E
J O H N N Y J U M P U P .
. G E O . P I A N O S
. Q U E E N A N N E S L A C E
A T T A R . N E O N . L U T E
R I N S E . I A G O . O R E M
S P E E D . E T O N . R U T S
```

49

```
M E S S ■ A T R A ■ L I K E D
A B U T ■ C H O P ■ U T H E R
C A P O ■ R E A L ■ T I A R A
K N E W T O O M U C H ■ K I M
■ ■ R E D S ■ ■ S P E C I E S
R A N ■ S T E P ■ A R I ■ ■ ■
U F O S ■ I D E A ■ A R G U E
L O V E D C A T D A N C I N G
E R A T O ■ M E A N ■ A N D A
■ ■ O W L ■ R Y A N ■ G O D ■
C H U N N E L ■ C E D E ■ ■ ■
R I N ■ F E L L T O E A R T H
E V I T A ■ A E O N ■ R A R E
P E T A L ■ M E N D ■ I L I A
E D S E L ■ A R E A ■ N E X T
```

50

```
V I V A ■ D O O M ■ P H O T O
A D E N ■ E B R O ■ T E N O R
N I N E ■ P E E N ■ B R O M O
Y O U W H O Y O O H O O ■ ■ ■
A T E ■ A S S ■ L E A D C A R
■ ■ ■ D R E ■ M I S T ■ O L E
A S H E S ■ O A T S ■ A L O E
C H E K H O V C H E C K O F F
R O L E ■ P E A S ■ H I N T S
E V E ■ F A R O ■ F I N ■ ■ ■
S E N I O R S ■ L O N ■ S S E
■ M Y T H A I M A I T A I ■ ■
B A T H E ■ O G L E ■ B O R E
O N A I R ■ O R A N ■ A L A I
W A R P S ■ T A C T ■ R E N O
```

51

```
T E M ■ M O L A R ■ M A R C O
U S E ■ A B U S E ■ U N H A T
R C A ■ B E L I E ■ D O E R S
B O N N E Y L A D D ■ N O R ■
O R I E L ■ ■ S U E ■ S L O ■
S T E E L E R S ■ O R A T O R
■ ■ ■ T A O S ■ I R A T E ■ ■
■ L E A K E Y F A W C E T T ■
F O L L Y ■ S I N K ■ ■ ■ ■ ■
D W E L L S ■ A S S E R T E D
R E V ■ E E L ■ ■ L E A V E ■
■ G A L ■ W I L D E O A T E S
G E T I T ■ N A O M I ■ E N T
A R O M A ■ E L L I S ■ R U R
P E R O N ■ N O L T E ■ S P Y
```

52

```
R O M P ■ P E T E ■ T A B O O
E R I E ■ A L E X ■ R E R U N
D I N E ■ D I C T ■ I R A T E
C O O K E D T H E B O O K S ■
A L A ■ R Y E ■ R I D ■ E M S
P E N T A ■ S P I C E ■ M A O
■ ■ U S A ■ R O E ■ S E R B ■
D U S T E D F O R P R I N T S
U N O S ■ D A N ■ S E Z ■ ■ ■
D R Y ■ H E L G A ■ A E S O P
S O S ■ A N D ■ V O L ■ E R E
■ L A U N D E R E D M O N E Y
F L U N G ■ R A N D ■ P O G O
R E C T O ■ A G U E ■ T R O T
O D E O N ■ L E E R ■ S A N E
```

53

```
N O P A R ■ L E S T ■ I S I N
O R A T E ■ E T T A ■ A T N O
G O G O D A N C E R ■ N A T L
■ E N O L A ■ N O D ■ R A E ■
D O D O ■ Y O Y O T R I C K S
A L O F T ■ L U G ■ A S H E S
N E W ■ E R I C ■ S S N ■ ■ ■
■ N O N O N A N E T T E ■ ■ ■
■ ■ H A T ■ T O N I ■ V A N ■
A G A I N ■ D A S ■ C H I V E
C O C O C H A N E L ■ O L E O
T E T ■ Y A K ■ C D R O M ■ ■
U S S R ■ S O S O R E V I E W
A T A D ■ I T O N ■ M E N S A
L O S S ■ T A T E ■ O R D E R
```

54

```
C A S A ■ S T A C Y ■ C Z A R
O P E L ■ L A T H E ■ O I S E
N E L L ■ A R T I S T S P A D
I A M S A M S A M I A M ■ ■ ■
C R A W L ■ U R N ■ D I S K S
■ ■ E G G S ■ E N A C T E D ■
■ A D L A I ■ B Y E ■ E L S ■
■ C A L L M E I S H M A E L ■
A T L ■ M N O ■ R E P L Y ■ ■
G O A T E E D ■ B U M P ■ ■ ■
T R I A L ■ G E R ■ O L S E N
■ M Y N A M E I S E A R L ■ ■
M A K E S A M I N T ■ P U R E
A X I S ■ N E R D S ■ I T O R
T E X T ■ A S S A Y ■ E E L S
```

55

```
G E M . A M A S S . S P I R E
O R E . R U P E E . A U R A L
F I R S T S E E D . G N O M E
O C C U L T . T A O . C N B C
R A I S E . D O N T S H O O T
. . I S P Y . . T R I X .
P I P E S T E M . S N I P E
C A L . . A R U B A . D E L
S N A R E . . G O L D L E A F
. Y U K S . N E A L .
G I M M E A B U D . N A T C H
R O O M . W A R . I G N O R E
A N N A N . M A Y F L O W E R
S I E G E . B L A S E . E A T
P A Y E E . A S T O R . D M Z
```

56

```
M E N S A . P I T T . R E D O
A T O L L . E C H O . A V E R
T O N E D . C H U R C H I L L
A N O D E . . A M E R . T H O
. . . G R E A T B R I T A I N
F I R E M A N . . S O B S . .
L O O . E S T A . . . A S T A
A T L A N T I C C H A R T E R
B A L I . . T O E S . A R I
. . N C A A . L A S A G N A
U N I T E D S T A T E S . .
N O D . D E S I . . S H E B A
R O O S E V E L T . S O W E R
I S L E . I R E D . E R E C T
P E S T . L T D S . D E S K S
```

57

```
L H A S A . G A S P . S C A T
B O L O S . O M A R . I O T A
S N I F F . L A C E . G L O P
. G E T O F F T H E P H O N E
. . P R O . E N O . N E D
F L O E . N Y E T . L A Y S
C O R D . D U G . P A C .
C L E A N U P Y O U R R O O M
. L E E . P O R . O K R A
. G O S H . A T O P . P S S T
A R F . R O W . L A H .
D O Y O U R H O M E W O R K
E C O N . L I M O . I B E A M
P E R M . O L I O . L I S L E
T R E E . N E T S . L A T E R
```

58

```
A M M O . P D A S . O C T E T
R E A P . A R N O . F L O R A
T A K E M Y W O R D F O R I T
S T E N O . A N T I . A N N A
. . . H O S T . O K O K . .
P A G O D A S . F E B . A F T
A C L U . R O T . I N T E R
T R U S T I N W H A T I S A Y
S I T E S . O A R . N E T S
Y D S . P E A . M I D E A S T
. . U S S R . S A I L . .
G W E N . P A P A . M I D A S
Y O U C A N B E L I E V E M E
M O R A L . I R A Q . E M I T
S L O P E . C U D S . S O D S
```

59

```
S T E M . U R I S . J A F A R
L A V A . P E C K . A T E I N
A L A I . T R E E . G R A D S
P E N T H O U S E S U I T E .
. . R A I N . . H A S H . .
O D D E S T . B E E R K E G S
F R I D A . F O L D . . R O I
F I R S T C L A S S C A B I N
T E T . H A T E . A T O N E
O D Y S S E Y S . I D T A G S
. T O E S . . I N R E .
. F R O N T R O W C E N T E R
S L I T S . A B O O . D E L I
C A C H E . M I N D . E X E C
I N K E D . P E T E . E T C H
```

60

```
M I C E . M A I M S . R A J A
A S E A . A R D E N . E V E R
R E N T . N E E D L E W O R K
X E S . K I T E D . T A N K S
. . O P R A H . L A H R . .
H U R R I C A N E L A M P .
E S S E S . E R I N . L O A
A S H Y . T O A S T . P A I L
T R I . S H U T . S A Y N O
. P O T A T O P A N C A K E
. N E I L . E D I T S .
A B I D E . A E S O P . C O E
F A C E P O W D E R . S E X Y
A L E C . T R I T E . K N E E
R I S K . B Y E A R . Y E N S
```

61

J	E	F	F	■	S	P	A	T	■	P	A	W	A	T
O	P	I	E	■	H	U	G	O	■	A	S	I	D	E
G	E	N	T	L	E	B	E	N	■	R	I	N	D	S
S	E	N	I	O	R	■	R	E	D	C	R	O	S	S
■	■	D	E	P	P	■	■	W	E	E	■	■	■	■
O	P	T	■	W	A	R	M	W	E	L	C	O	M	E
C	R	O	W	S	■	F	A	I	L	■	A	N	O	N
T	I	K	I	■	L	I	S	Z	T	■	L	E	N	D
E	D	E	N	■	U	R	S	A	■	B	L	U	T	O
T	E	N	D	E	R	M	E	R	C	Y	■	P	E	W
■	■	C	R	I	■	■	D	A	N	K	■	■	■	■
L	O	C	H	N	E	S	S	■	N	O	I	D	E	A
E	L	L	I	E	■	K	I	N	D	W	O	R	D	S
G	L	O	M	S	■	I	D	O	L	■	S	E	N	T
S	A	G	E	T	■	M	E	R	E	■	K	W	A	I

62

B	A	A	■	T	E	R	M	■	W	R	E	S	T	S
E	L	L	■	A	L	E	E	■	E	A	R	T	H	A
R	E	G	■	L	A	V	E	N	D	E	R	O	I	L
G	R	A	P	E	N	U	T	S	■	■	A	N	N	E
S	T	E	R	N	■	E	S	C	■	N	N	E	■	■
■	■	■	I	T	S	■	■	H	O	T	T	U	B	■
S	P	A	S	■	N	I	S	S	A	N	■	O	N	A
P	L	U	M	T	U	C	K	E	R	E	D	O	U	T
C	O	T	■	O	B	E	Y	E	D	■	E	L	M	S
A	D	O	P	T	S	■	■	Y	E	P	■	■	■	■
■	P	O	E	■	A	W	E	■	M	O	R	O	N	■
S	T	A	T	■	■	L	I	L	A	C	T	I	M	E
P	U	R	P	L	E	P	R	O	S	E	■	P	E	I
U	N	T	I	E	S	■	E	P	E	E	■	E	G	G
R	E	S	E	T	S	■	D	E	A	D	■	N	A	H

63

B	L	I	G	H	■	A	R	C	H	■	S	T	I	R
A	I	M	E	E	■	M	I	C	A	■	T	A	D	A
M	E	E	T	M	E	I	N	S	T	L	O	U	I	S
B	O	A	S	■	A	D	S	■	P	O	P	T	O	P
A	N	N	O	Y	S	■	E	M	I	R	S	■	■	■
■	■	R	E	E	D	■	I	N	D	U	T	C	H	■
S	L	E	E	P	L	E	S	S	■	S	P	R	A	Y
K	A	T	■	S	C	O	U	T	■	■	O	L	D	■
I	D	T	A	G	■	I	N	S	E	A	T	T	L	E
S	E	E	S	R	E	D	■	E	S	A	I	■	■	■
■	■	A	I	M	E	D	■	T	R	E	M	O	R	■
D	E	A	R	M	E	■	U	K	E	■	D	O	R	A
A	U	T	U	M	N	I	N	N	E	W	Y	O	R	K
U	R	A	L	■	D	R	N	O	■	E	E	R	I	E
B	O	D	E	■	S	K	E	W	■	E	D	E	N	S

64

E	A	S	E	■	B	O	O	N	S	■	T	H	A	T
B	L	O	C	■	R	A	D	I	O	■	H	O	P	S
B	A	D	H	A	I	R	D	A	Y	■	A	R	I	E
■	■	■	O	N	E	■	C	A	B	I	N	E	T	■
I	N	P	E	N	■	T	R	I	■	A	L	E	C	S
L	A	O	S	■	S	A	N	D	R	A	D	E	E	■
L	I	L	■	D	I	A	L	■	I	B	N	■	■	■
■	L	I	V	E	F	R	E	E	O	R	D	I	E	■
O	A	S	■	I	L	S	A	■	■	D	A	B	■	■
P	L	A	Y	D	O	U	G	H	■	T	O	R	O	■
A	U	R	A	E	■	P	H	I	■	J	O	L	L	Y
T	R	I	G	R	A	M	■	C	O	W	■	■	■	■
R	I	S	E	■	P	O	S	T	A	G	E	D	U	E
I	N	T	R	■	E	S	T	E	S	■	R	O	S	A
A	G	A	S	■	S	T	Y	L	E	■	S	T	A	R

65

A	V	E	C	■	S	T	R	A	W	■	S	Y	N	C
H	I	L	O	■	P	R	A	D	A	■	H	E	A	L
A	V	E	R	■	R	E	P	E	L	■	R	O	S	A
B	A	C	K	B	A	Y	■	L	E	E	W	A	Y	■
■	■	T	O	N	S	■	S	P	E	W	■	■	■	■
A	D	D	I	N	G	■	B	I	L	L	D	A	N	A
W	I	E	L	D	■	O	N	U	S	■	S	E	M	■
A	X	L	E	■	S	L	A	N	G	■	S	C	A	B
S	I	T	■	I	N	O	R	■	P	E	A	R	L	■
H	E	A	D	C	O	L	D	■	E	L	A	P	S	E
■	■	H	O	W	L	■	A	X	E	L	■	■	■	■
V	A	C	A	N	T	■	S	I	D	E	B	E	T	■
I	G	O	R	■	I	M	A	C	S	■	V	O	T	E
S	E	A	M	■	R	O	B	O	T	■	E	R	O	S
A	S	T	A	■	E	T	A	T	S	■	L	E	N	T

66

D	I	T	C	H	■	B	O	G	■	Q	U	I	E	T
I	T	A	L	O	■	A	D	O	■	U	L	T	R	A
G	S	U	I	T	■	B	O	A	■	E	N	T	E	R
I	M	P	O	S	T	E	R	T	U	N	A	■	■	■
N	E	E	■	E	A	R	■	E	M	T	■	T	E	A
■	■	■	M	A	T	U	R	E	P	I	N	O	T	S
■	A	G	I	T	A	T	E	■	■	N	E	W	A	T
E	T	N	A	■	S	H	I	L	L	■	V	E	T	O
S	W	A	M	P	■	■	G	O	O	B	E	R	S	■
P	A	T	I	O	M	U	N	S	T	E	R	■	■	■
Y	R	S	■	T	A	N	■	E	S	T	■	K	I	A
■	■	■	P	E	R	M	U	T	A	T	I	O	N	S
S	U	S	A	N	■	A	R	I	■	O	M	A	N	I
A	N	T	I	C	■	D	I	M	■	R	I	L	E	D
C	O	Y	L	Y	■	E	S	E	■	S	N	A	R	E

67

```
B A T H . . B A W L . I N C A
A L A I . G E N R E . D E A R
S I L L . M E D E A . L A N K
H E L L O S T R A N G E R . .
. N Y E T . E T T A . B A Y .
. L O O K W H O S H E R E . .
S T S . R E S . P O E M S . .
H A N D G U N . N O S I R E E
A B O I L . R A W . S D S . .
H O W V E Y O U B E E N . . .
S O P . N O U N . O O P S . .
. L O N G T I M E N O S E E .
C M O N . U L N A S . D E A L
H O W L . R A T S O . L U L L
I T S Y . T W O S . E D Y S .
```

68

```
M A C S . O R K I N . K U R D
I T U P . S O A M I . I R O N
N E L L . H I T O N . E S T A
C A P I T A L O F J A V A . .
E R A T O . . F A Q . M A G .
. . . M I C E . . U S A I R .
A R S . B R O A D W A Y J O E
S H A G . A T R I A . R O L E
C O M P A N Y P E R K . R I D
A D M A N . S U M O . . . . .
P A Y . T A S . C H A K A . .
. S T I C K I N T H E M U D .
Z O O S . C E D A R . M I D I
I L S A . T I L D E . A T O M
P E A R . S N E A K . N Y S E
```

69

```
S P A R . W O O D S . P R E K
L E G O . A B B I E . R O T E
A R E A . D E I S M . A O N E
B U D D H I S T H O L Y M A N
. . . S A N E . L E S . . . .
S A W I N G . M A I D . C A W
P R I D E . B A R N . M O P E
A N D E S P A C K A N I M A L
M I E S . O D E S . E N A C T
S E N . A R E S . D A I S E S
. . A L T . D O T S . . . .
B L A Z E I N B R O O K L Y N
E A S T . C A R O M . I I I I
N I T E . O P I N E . R E N T
E R I C . S A T E D . T U G S
```

70

```
C R A G . S C U B A . B A A S
R O N A . E A S E L . L U L L
I B I S . W R E S T . O R L Y
B O M B O N B R O A D W A Y .
S T E A M . . S T R O P . . .
. . G A W K . . S T I F L E .
E A R . N A A C P . P L A Y .
S W A Y I N T H E B R E E Z E
S E G O . T I A R A . W E D .
O D E S S A . T A B S . . . .
. . E U R O S . . B O A T S .
. C O M E D I A N W I L S O N
S A K I . E L S I E . V I N E
A L I T . N E S T S . E D G E
G L E E . T R Y S T . S E A R
```

71

```
C L A N . S C A R F . E N D S
Y A L E . L O W E R . V I E W
S T O W . I N A N E . I N C A
T H E T I M E Y O U E N J O Y
. . O N L Y . D E C A Y S . .
E V E N L Y . P A I N E . . .
M E N S A . A U R A . S A S S
I N C . W A S T I N G . M A O
L I E U . R E I D . E P O X Y
. . P E C A N . S L A K E S .
M O O L A H . S T I R . . . .
I S N O T W A S T E D T I M E
N A S A . A W A R E . I D O L
E K E D . Y O K E L . N E S S
R A T S . S L E W S . G A T E
```

72

```
S T U D . G E N A . A G N E W
H Y P O . O L A V . L E A S H
O P E N . S O M E . B E T S Y
P E N E L O P E C R U Z . . .
S A N T A F E . E M E R I L .
. . H U T . T I L . R O T O .
I D T A G . M O T I F . S S R
S O U T H S E A S C R U I S E
L O G . S H A D Y . O N E O N
A N A T . A N Y . O L D . . .
M E T E O R . T R I E S T E .
. C L E A N U P C R E W S . .
M O T H S . R O S H . A L I T
A N N I E . A N K A . G E N E
E A T E N . B O S N . E S S E
```

73

```
C B S . . V O I C E . C O M P
A U T O . I N C A S . O M A R
S N A P . P U E R T O R I C O
A C T R E S S . H A U N T E D
S H E A R . . S O T S . . . .
. . T H E M U P P E T S H O W
M E R . C A P E . . . T E M A
E L E C T R I C C O M P A N Y
O L E O . . T O T O . V I S .
W E S T S I D E S T O R Y . .
. . . E M E R . . S A L S A .
L A S C A L A . T H E R I T Z
R I T A M O R E N O . I N A T
O D E S . S I N U S . N E V E
N A P S . T E S T S . S E C .
```

74

```
M A R C H . W E L D . S E R B
O C A L A . I S E E . T R I O
C H R I S T M A S W R E A T H
K E E P . O P U S . E N T E R
. . . J A R S . O H N O . . .
A N T O N Y . S N I T . F A N
N O H I T . G O O F . G A Z E
K W A N Z A A U N I T Y C U P
L I N T . I N R E . O P E R A
E N E . O R G S . V E S S E L
. . W I S P . T I D Y . . . .
S C I O N . L O I N . M A R T
H A N U K K A H M E N O R A H
A T T N . A N T E . A T O N E
M O O D . T K O S . P H O T O
```

75

```
A B L E . L A T H E . C R A M
R A I N . A C R E S . L A N E
A B C D A Y T I M E H O S T S
B E E . N M E X . O S H E A .
. . M I A . M A R E . . . . .
. F I L M N O M I N A T I O N
L A D L E . D O L E S . L B O
E R L E . G E T I T . V O I D
A G E . D O N E E . Z E S T S
F O R M E R S T U D E N T S .
. . A L E E . O L D . . . . .
B E A S T . B A N D . S H A .
A L P H A B E T Q U A R T E T
E L E E . A L E U T . E U R O
R E D S . T I N A S . A D A M
```

The New York Times

Crossword Puzzles

The #1 Name in Crosswords

Available at your local bookstore or online at nytimes.com/nytstore

St. Martin's Griffin